Jo

Introduction
and Study
Guide

T&T CLARK STUDY GUIDES TO THE NEW TESTAMENT

Series Editor

Tat-siong Benny Liew, College of the Holy Cross, USA

Other titles in the series include

1&2 Thessalonians: An Introduction and Study Guide

1 Peter: An Introduction and Study Guide

2 Corinthians: An Introduction and Study Guide

Colossians: An Introduction and Study Guide

Ephesians: An Introduction and Study Guide

Galatians: An Introduction and Study Guide

Hebrews: An Introduction and Study Guide

James: An Introduction and Study Guide

John: An Introduction and Study Guide

Luke: An Introduction and Study Guide

Mark: An Introduction and Study Guide

Matthew: An Introduction and Study Guide

Philemon: An Introduction and Study Guide

Philippians: An Introduction and Study Guide

Romans: An Introduction and Study Guide

The Letters of Jude and Second Peter: An Introduction and Study Guide

T&T Clark Study Guides to the Old Testament

1 & 2 Samuel: An Introduction and Study Guide

1 & 2 Kings: An Introduction and Study Guide

Ecclesiastes: An Introduction and Study Guide

Exodus: An Introduction and Study Guide

Ezra-Nehemiah: An Introduction and Study Guide

Leviticus: An Introduction and Study Guide

Jeremiah: An Introduction and Study Guide

Job: An Introduction and Study Guide

Joshua: An Introduction and Study Guide

Psalms: An Introduction and Study Guide

Song of Songs: An Introduction and Study Guide

Numbers: An Introduction and Study Guide

John: An Introduction and Study Guide

History, Community, and Ideology

Francisco Lozada Jr.

t&tclark

LONDON · NEW YORK · OXFORD · NEW DELHI · SYDNEY

T&T CLARK
Bloomsbury Publishing Plc
50 Bedford Square, London, WC1B 3DP, UK
1385 Broadway, New York, NY 10018, USA

BLOOMSBURY, T&T CLARK and the T&T Clark logo are trademarks of
Bloomsbury Publishing Plc

First published in Great Britain 2018

A catalogue record for this book is available from the British Library.

A catalog record for this book is available from the Library of Congress.

ISBN: HB: 978-0-5676-9284-9
PB: 978-0-5676-7487-6
ePDF: 978-0-5676-7488-3
ePUB: 978-0-5676-7489-0

Typeset by Newgen KnowledgeWorks Pvt. Ltd., Chennai, India
Printed and bound in Great Britain

To find out more about our authors and books visit www.bloomsbury.com
and sign up for our newsletters.

In Memoriam
Charles Fischer
(1926–2017)

Contents

Preface ix

Introduction 1

1 **John's Historical Background** 11

The Rootedness of John 11
The Historical Identity of John: Fixed and/or Fluid 13
References 26
Further Reading 27

2 **John's Literary Background: Plot** 29

Narrative of Unsettlement (1:1-18) 32
Narrative of Travel/Crossing (1:19–17:26) 35
Narrative of Resettlement (18:1–21:25) 49
References 53
Further Reading 54

3 **John's Characterization: "The Jews," Women, and the World** 55

"The Jews" 57
Women in the Gospel 61
The World 69
References 70
Further Reading 72

4 **John 1:1-18: A World Split Apart** 73

Introduction 74
At Home—The World Above: 1:1-2 74
The Word's Crossing: 1:3-17 76
Returning Home—The World Above: 1:18 82

Conclusion 83
References 84
Further Reading 84

5   John 17:1-26: A Prayer for Unity and Community 85

Introduction 86
Jesus Prays for Himself (17:1-5) 87
Jesus Prays for His Disciples (17:6-19) 89
Jesus Prays for All Believers (17:20-26) 92
Conclusion 94
Further Reading 96

Conclusion: John, the "Maverick" Gospel—Revisited 97

Bibliography 101
Author Index 107
Biblical Index 109
Subject Index 115

Preface

This brief volume is written with a didactic and scholarly intent. What this means is that the volume grows out of a course on John that I teach at Brite Divinity School. The course aims to study John from a literary and ideological perspective, informed by a sociohistorical orientation. The course also allows me to explore what it means to do a literary and ideological reading of John, thus with an aim to encourage other Johannine interpreters to consider some of the questions that I propose in this volume. I regard both these aims strongly informed by my interest in the history of hermeneutics and historiography that underlies this volume. Understanding the process of how we come to produce meaning, at least for me, helps explain how the world then and now plays a role in the construction of knowledge. They are also informed by my interest in US Latino/a history and culture. For example, how the history of the US Southwest borderlands is read and understood influences, like John does, the representation of the "other"—those minoritized groups who are ascribed undesirable representation and assignment to inferior positions by dominant groups (Castles and Miller 2009: 35). For me, there is a connection between scholarship and political or theological responsibility.

This volume is a glimpse into my past interpretative approach, my present approach, and my future approach: past in the sense that I still hold onto the principle of allowing the text to speak for itself (at least I am aiming for this), present in the sense that one cannot do scholarship in isolation from contemporary questions, and future in the sense that how we write the past (historiography) is important to how we see the future or read John in the future. This hermeneutical perspective owes much to not only students who have questioned me in the classroom but also colleagues such as James Duke, with whom I have co-taught the course "History of Hermeneutics" on two occasions. Thank you, Jim, for your collegiality, editorial suggestions, and critical hermeneutical insights in and out of the classroom.

The volume is written not only for students but also for those scholars interested in seeing one among many ideological readings of John. The volume does not include footnotes, but it does reference some scholars where I think it is important to do so. There are other studies in the field of hermeneutics that have also informed my thinking over the years. Such works/authors are not repetitively cited but they include Hans-Georg Gadamer (1979), Michel-Roth Trouillot (1995), R. Alan Culpepper (1998), Adele Reinhartz (2001), and Fernando F. Segovia (2000, 2015). Segovia's works have been quite influential on my understanding of historiography and is reflected throughout the volume.

A good example of Segovia's influence is my understanding of all readers as interpreters, not just public or scholarly readers. Thus, the word "interpreters" will be used throughout the volume to reference all readers. Also, the Gospel of John is referenced in different ways: the Fourth Gospel, John, or the Gospel of John. Sometimes I use the word "text" to refer to all of it and sometimes "text" means a particular verse or unit. The context will inform the word's meaning or usage.

Like all volumes, this one is approached from a certain theoretical and methodological orientation. I label my approach literary-ideological or literary and ideological perspective. Similar to a phoropter at an optometrist's office, many lenses can be flipped back and forth to search for the best vision ("Is it better with 1 or with 2?"). This volume also employs a literary and ideological lens or perspective to look for the best vision based on the questions at hand, but it is not the only vision. It is simply one among many theoretical and methodological approaches out there. The literary-ideological representative readings I do provide in this volume do not go into depth, but they give interpreters a taste of what it might look like and, perhaps, the incentive to do it their own way.

The project has been a joy to work on and I am grateful to all those who have made this volume possible, especially Charles Fischer for whom my teaching position is named. I am also grateful to Tat-siong Benny Liew of the College of Holy Cross who invited me to contribute to the series and who provided valuable feedback on the volume. And finally, I would also like to thank Dr. Cathy L. Roan for her editorial advice.

In closing, quotations from John, unless otherwise noted, are from the New Revised Standard Version (NRSV). Also, after each chapter, I provide not only a list of studies that informed my writing of that chapter but also references for further reading.

References

Castles, S., and M. J. Miller (2009), *The Age of Migration*, 4th ed.
    New York: Guilford Press.

Culpepper, R. A. (1998), *The Gospel and Letters of John*, Nashville: Abingdon.

Gadamer, H.-G. (1979), *Truth and Method*, trans. W. Glen-Doepel, ed.
    J. Cumming and G. Barden, 2nd ed. London: Sheed and Ward.

Reinhartz, A. (2001), *Befriending the Beloved Disciple*, New York: Continuum.

Segovia, F. F. (2000), *Decolonizing Biblical Studies*, Maryknoll, NY:
    Orbis Books.

Segovia, F. F. (2015), "Criticism in Critical Times: Reflections on Vision and
    Task," *Journal of Biblical Literature* 134, no. 1: 671–95.

Trouillot, M.-R. (1995), *Silencing the Past: Power and the Production of History*,
    Boston: Beacon Press.

Introduction

This introductory volume is written with a focus on hermeneutics or interpretation. Questions about how John is read, understood, and applied inform this volume. In so doing, the volume raises an overarching though implicit question: How do interpreters (including myself) come to understand John? This central question is threaded through the entire volume. Chapter 1 explores how general historical information about John is constructed. Chapter 2 introduces how the plot of John is delimited. Chapter 3 analyzes how characterization in John is produced. Chapters 4 and 5 provide representative literary–ideological readings of John. All in all, each chapter is informed by the underlying question of how we come to an understanding of John, given that John is a text written many years ago—as those involved in the narrativization of history through story did so in a distant past (with the exception of modern-day interpreters). Accordingly, I see this line of questioning calling for an ideological approach, which is the methodological orientation that informs this volume's reading of John.

An ideological approach to John can be done in many ways, but what drives many ideological readings of text is the study of how meaning (no matter how it is constructed or construed) serves to sustain and legitimate systems of power. Ideology refers to the ways meaning (or representation) justifies and sustains dominant and privileged relations and being (Thompson 1984: 11; 198). For this volume, I am interested in how ideological meaning is constructed by way of cultural expressions emanating from the narrative itself in its final form. How a text (or for that matter a visual image, object, or event) describes or depicts something (e.g., the cosmos, the Johannine community, God) and through its narrative conjures up in one's mind's eye a mental representation of the word (or image, object, event) for which one interprets what that representation means, and thus influences or regulates one's relationship (or behavior) toward that representation. For instance, take the contested phrase "illegal immigrant." The phrase constructs a negative mental representation of immigrants and thus potentially influences one's relationship to and thinking about "illegal immigrants." If you take an example from John, the text, "You are from your father the devil" (8:44a), correlates "you" with "the Jews," which is the antecedent of "you," with "the devil," thus constructing a portrayal of "evil Jews" in readers' minds. Such a representation of "the Jews" is not static. It produces an image of "the Jews" that is consumed by readers and listeners across time and place, thus regulating the behavior of non-Jews toward "the Jews" or Jewish people, as has been witnessed throughout history. Without a doubt, terminology for groups defines groups both politically and epistemologically (Trouillot 1995: 115). Of course, the context (historical and narrative) of such words must be taken into consideration as well as the sources or authors who spoke or wrote those words in constructing meaning. Nonetheless, an ideological approach, as I employ it, is interested in understanding how such an ideological process works through readings of John and what might be its effects.

 More specifically, my ideological approach is joined with a narrative approach, with a focus on the text's words, syntax, and order—or what is sometimes called a close-reading approach. It is not the only approach but one that argues for and makes meanings from how the narrative is rhetorically crafted. My narrative approach also explores characterization in relationship to representation. Examining the words and actions of the characters and how characters engage other characters is another form of close reading that I use in this volume.

My ideological approach challenges any notion that the representation that exists through interpretation does not or should not reflect the relationships between peoples or communities in the world today (Lozada 2002). Although many interpreters aim to use the text like a mirror—to reflect the representation of the narrative as if it still exists today—or appeal to the intent of the author as the sole authority of what a text means, an ideological reading of a text such as John is significant because it focuses on the process of how representation is constructed. The assumption here is that such representations of the narrative world of John have real social effects on social behavior, whether or not one has different stakes in the narrative, for whatever reason. The text (John) is not just an ecclesial document; it is also a public document that calls for engagement, like all public "sacred" documents. A good example of this is the Museum of the Bible in Washington, DC. The museum aims, among others, to offer another narrative of the beginnings of the United States with the intent to show that the initial stages of the United States correlate with a divinely providential narrative of the beginning of creation (https://www.museumofthebible.org/exhibits/bible-in-america). The linkage between the various exhibits and representation is surely controlling (like all museums and exhibits do) the gaze of the eye, but it also has the potential to influence people's thinking (or belief) and, consequently, social behavior.

It is this politics through representation of worldviews that I am interested in exploring, because my particular hermeneutics is less about what John means and more about how meaning is constructed. This is what drives my hermeneutics. Such a line of thinking was missing in the history of biblical hermeneutics, including Johannine studies, for many years. From the 1800s to the present, what drove Johannine studies was an interest in a positivistic type of historicity based on the rules of Western epistemology, conventions, and procedures. That is, the driving question was "what happened" that gave rise to the writing of John (and it has remained so among many practitioners). Questions about where John was written, when it was written, who wrote it, and the events that led to its composition guided many Johannine scholars' research agendas. To be fair, these scholars were simply following the rules established by the educated elite of the academy or legislators of the guild on constructing knowledge. Such rules continue to be passed down, including by me, to students in the classroom.

Such questions are indeed important to ask, for they place John within a particular historical context with the aim to better understand John as the first readers/hearers could understand—but this is a challenge to reconstruct. Such an approach allows the text of John to have a voice, that is, as the assumption goes. The aim of historical interpretation is to root John in its historical context in its own time and place. The rules are informed by a Western epistemology and scientific approach (observation, collection of data, testing) that builds on the work of previous scholarship; it aims to reconstruct a history of a layered text by looking at the collection of selective sources (source criticism), the cutting and pasting of such sources in some order (form criticism), and the editing of the order to rebuild the layered history of the text (redaction criticism). The mental image of John is like an archeological tell; scholars excavate the many layers to report on "what happened" that gave rise to the final form. What is seldom discussed, in what is known in the academic guild as the historical–critical approach to the study of biblical texts, is that the selection of sources, the cataloguing of literary forms, or even the redaction process of such material is selective and an act of power. Sources, forms, and redactions are not neutral (Trouillot 2015: 48); someone with a particular point of view created the source, selected the forms, and edited the material. What is more, someone with a point of view narrates the final form and someone (the flesh-and-blood interpreter) with a point of view interprets such a narrative. At the end, what one does with a text (or John) is a narrativization of a selective history at all levels (Lozada 2006). It is very similar, if I may, to when one reads the history of the United States as a history that began with the *Mayflower* or a history that began with immigration. The selective process of the actors involved in such a history as well as that of the historians who aim to tell this history will influence the narrativization of the history. The analogy is not perfect, but understanding the process of how interpreters reach the point of "that which is said to have happened" is important in understanding how meaning is constructed. To be fair to historically oriented interpreters, the same can be said about literary interpreters. For instance, the selection of certain words and syntax, or delineating a narrative order in a certain way, is also a particular process. At the end, all approaches to a text like John are incomplete, no matter how many pages one composes. In a commentary or monograph based on "empirical" facts or "authoritative" voices, the approximation of "what happened" is simply that, an approximation or, as I tell my students, a "sketch."

What is overlooked many times by even the best practitioners of biblical studies is a critical retrospection of how they reached "that which is said to have happened" (Trouillot 1995: 1–4). There is less focus on the sociohistorical process of constructing a history or a narrative or an interpretation of John. The result is a one-sided history or narrative that is sent across time and place, as with the case below with the circumstances of John's composition proposed by Martyn and Brown (see Chapter 1). There is no mention of the role of the interpreters or their subjectivity in the construction of a history, for instance, or no critical reflection on the process by which they reached "that which is said to have happened" in the Johannine community, leaving readers with the impression that they were present at the time of composition or the impression that they are omniscient scholars. Again, such scholars are simply following the rules of the academic guild or the modernist impulse of their time in constructing knowledge influenced by nineteenth-century hermeneutics that still has great influence on our understanding of texts today.

As alluded to above, the same lack of attention to the process of settling on "that which is said to have happened" through story is also true of literary critics, particularly in the 1990s. Traditionally, the dominant questions focus on what the story is about and how the story is told (discourse), accompanied by rhetorical matters (e.g., plot development or rhetorical devices such as irony) and reader-response questions such as the role of the reader—implied, inscribed, or real—during the reading process of a text in constructing meaning. Literary criticism, particularly along the lines of narrative criticism, presents a one-sided narrative of or about John. Very little discussion on the process of narrativization occurs, with the exception of some scholars sensitively aware of the particularity of their social location. Keep in mind, this turn to literary criticism (as well as other forms of criticism) does not mean that historical questions ceased: on the contrary, they are alive and well but the conditions of the times with regard to the process of meaning push against the dominant modes of criticism, thus opening the door for other questions and approaches to John. For instance, the field of Johannine studies (and biblical studies in general), with the influence of postmodernism in the early 1990s, began to question the dominant principles of universality and positivism at play in the construction of meaning. Meaning is no longer seen as static or something to be recovered; rather, it is seen as a construction or a creation between the text and the reader, so to speak. Within this understanding, readers move into visibility and can no longer hide behind a veil of positivist history or neutral objectivity. Meaning is no longer definitive but open to scrutiny. This does not mean that such an epistemological development is without problems. For instance, most interpreters, including myself, who embrace this development, seldom give a sustained, critical account of how their subjectivity informs their production of meaning. This meaning-making process is simply not part of the dominant rules of the academic game (in the Western world). Again, this does not mean that meaning itself, as a repository of undistorted events of early Johannine history or the life of the historical Jesus in John, ceased to be embraced by interpreters of John. For them, it is not a concern that the retrieval of meaning from the past is done from the present. However, the past world of John is only the past world of John because there is a present world reading and (in)forming the writing of that past world. The past is always written from the present (Trouillot 1995: 15).

With this principle, I turn to an ideological approach to John. I do so not because I do not see any value in the study of the historical world of John (which I would argue is still pertinent), but because my questions are more interested in how meaning is constructed in John. It is important to note that the study of early Christianity as represented in the New Testament is problematic. As the majority of commentaries attest, the lack of information identifying certain general historical information on John's background makes meaning difficult to reconstruct. Compared to other literary traditions, the sociohistorical information on John is at best an approximation, given its complex development as a composition and the lack of sources from 2,000 years ago (Miller 1993: 11; Segovia 2007: 161; Tolbert 2013: 20). Because of the poverty of sources behind the world of John, what happens most of the time—I am including my own work here—is simply a repositioning of those sources to generate a new narrative about John. Many scholars even cut across the canonical and noncanonical texts to cite as many other texts as possible (see their footnotes or endnotes) as a way to prove that what they have said is also said or alluded to in other texts. It is a moment of "fact" assembly in order to construct a narrative. We (in the West) all do it! It is part of the rules of the game. An ideological approach aims to provide a moment of being retrospective about how we do it. This is the added step to finding sources, assembling them, writing a narrative, and then interpreting this narrative. Such a step underpins this volume.

For example, in the sociohistorical field of Johannine scholarship such as empire studies, one traditional methodological step is to study John as if it were written from Ephesus (Asia Minor). Such a move is quite valuable because it places the reader in a hermeneutical place—though an imaginary one!—to understand something different, to walk in the shoes of another, if you will. In a sense it is an epistemological move that museums, films, and historical sites employ to take people's imaginations into the past with the hope of a better understanding of that past. Much attention by empire studies is given to why Ephesus was where John was composed, but less attention is given to why this tradition concluded "that which is said to have happened" happened in Ephesus, not to mention why an interpreter would want to hold on to this tradition. Again, I am not arguing whether John was written in Ephesus or not. I am suggesting that an extra step in understanding how such a move is made exposes the silent operation of power. This is what an ideological approach is after. Sources are not neutral; nor are the collectors of such sources or their interpreters. Such a move adds to our understanding of how the reconstruction of Johannine history works and why some of the history is thematized and some of it remains in silence.

Reconstructing the history of the Johannine text is important, but because of the challenge of securing sources and the repositioning of such sources to create a narrative, I prefer to focus more on the text in its final form. The text is a cultural expression of the world it came out of; that was a world in the shadow of (Roman) imperialism. As a cultural expression, John proposes a worldview, but that worldview is only accessible to us through interpretation—that is to say, that worldview is constructed through an interpreter's interaction with the text. In this sense, it is an ideological product that is a reflection of this encounter; this production or representation of the Johannine world—no matter how abstract—informs, in turn, how readers/hearers engage John, including their mental representation of the world and their behavior toward others in the world. The clearest example here, as I will show in the volume, is how the narrative constructs two worlds: a world above and a world below. Such a dualistic worldview influences how others, particularly unbelievers from the world below, are perceived and understood.

Several final points are in order here. The first is the role of myself as an interpreter. In this volume, I am thematizing questions of duality, movement, inclusion/exclusion because they inform the tension I experience in living in two cultures, as many individuals do in a variety of ways in society. It is a tension I carry within me as a US Latino, but a tension that provides me also with advantages. Living within two cultures (the dominant Anglo world and the Latino/a/x world) allows me to see both sides of the "border" (metaphorically speaking) and journey in both worlds through language and culture. Most importantly, embracing the tension of both worlds allows me to explore the differential exercise of power when worlds rub up against one another: between my world and John's world, between the world above and the world below, and between the world of insiders and the world of outsiders. Secondly, the approach I embrace here is simply a way to introduce readers to the study of John. It is not the only approach, but it is one that helps to focus on questions of representation as expressed through the narrative. It is not without its limits. To avoid engaging the sociohistorical world is problematic. I fully agree that meaning needs to be attached to its historical context. In this volume, I am simply choosing to focus on the narrative context as my primary entry point into John. Without a doubt, much of the general historical information appearing in Chapter 1 emanates from my own class notes, which is the collection of knowledge gained through reading the insightful commentaries, volumes, and studies over the years on John's historical background (see Chapter 1's bibliography). I may not cite them, but such studies do indeed inform my thinking. This also applies to the literary readings of John in Chapters 2 and 3. I may not always cite all the literary studies, but many of the contributions by Johannine literary scholars have also shaped my thinking about the narrative world of John (again, see the bibliography in these chapters). All of this is to say that I read John among a community of scholars, and that community guides my line of inquiry. Finally, a word about reading John in the twenty-first century: one of the key steps (as mentioned above) is to reflect critically on the process of constructing meaning—that is, in this volume's case, that which is said to have been constructed between the narrative and the interpreter. In so doing, in the last chapter of this volume (Conclusion), I shall provide a brief critical reflection on the effects and consequences of representation—its politics—vis-à-vis John's representation as the "Maverick Gospel."

References

Lozada Jr., F. (2002), "Contesting an Interpretation of John 5: Moving Beyond Colonial Evangelism," in M. W. Dube and J. L. Staley (eds.), *John and Postcolonialism: Travel, Space and Power*, The Bible and Postcolonialism, 7, 76–93, Sheffield: Sheffield Academic Press.

Lozada Jr., F. (2006), "Social Location and Johannine Scholarship: Looking Ahead," in F. Lozada Jr., and T. Thatcher (eds.), *New Currents through John: A Global Perspective*, 183–97, Atlanta: Society of Biblical Literature.

Miller, J. M. (1993), "Reading the Bible Historically: The Historian's Approach," in S. L. McKenzie and S. R. Haynes (eds.), *To Each Its Own Meaning: An Introduction to Biblical Criticism and Their Application*, 11–28, Louisville, KY: Westminster John Knox Press.

Segovia, F. F. (2007), "The Gospel of John," in F. F. Segovia and R. S. Sugirtharajah (eds.), *A Postcolonial Commentary on the New Testament Writings*, 156–93, Sheffield: Sheffield Academic Press.

Thompson, J. B. (1984), *Studies in the Theory of Ideology*, Cambridge: Polity Press.

Tolbert, M. A. (2013), "Writing History, Writing Culture, Writing Ourselves," in F. Lozada Jr. and Greg Carey (eds.), *Soundings in Cultural Criticism: Perspectives and Methods in Culture, Power, and Identity in the New Testament*, 17–30, Minneapolis, MN: Fortress Press.

Trouillot, M.-R. (1995), *Silencing the Past: Power and the Production of History*, Boston: Beacon Press. https://www.museumofthebible.org/exhibits/bible-in-america (accessed June 8, 2018).

Further Reading

Appleby, J., L. Hunt, and Margaret Jacob (1994), *Telling the Truth about History*, New York: W. W. Norton.

Bauman, Z. (1987), *Legislators and Interpreters*, Cambridge: Polity Press.

Benko, A. G. (2018), "Race in John: Racializing Discourse in the Fourth Gospel," PhD diss., Brite Divinity School.

Gadamer, H.-G. (1979), *Truth and Method*, 2nd ed., trans. W. Glen-Doepel, ed. J. Cumming and G. Barden, London: Sheed and Ward.

Jeanrond, W. (1994), *Theological Hermeneutics*, London: SCM Press.

Martínez, O. J. (1994), *Border People: Life and Society in the U.S.–Mexico Borderlands*, Arizona: University of Arizona Press.

Segovia, F. F. (2000), *Decolonizing Biblical Studies*, Maryknoll, NY: Orbis Books.

Segovia, F. F. (2015), "Criticism in Critical Times: Reflections on Vision and Task," *Journal of Biblical Literature* 134, no. 1: 671–95.

Taylor, C. (1994), *Multiculturalism: Examining the Politics of Recognition*, Princeton: Princeton University Press.

1

John's Historical Background

Chapter Outline

The Rootedness of John 11
The Historical Identity of John: Fixed and/or Fluid 13
References 26
Further Reading 27

The Rootedness of John

As early as the fifteenth and sixteenth centuries, scholars employed the hermeneutical principle of the "rootedness" of a text to uncover the historical background of the text and reveal its temporal, spatial, and historical situation. This early turn in the critical study of the Bible aided the educated, particularly ministers, in effective Christian preaching (Thiselton 2009: 22). The strategic entry point to the world of the text is to recover the historical situation of the text and, concomitantly, the intention of the author. This methodological tactic is still found today among diverse places: textbooks, predominantly with introductions to the Bible; historically oriented biblical commentaries; and, of course, in the classrooms at many academic departments (public and private) and theological schools. Behind this goal of bringing the text alive is the assumption that meaning exists in the world behind the text. The role of the interpreter is to paint a picture of what this ancient world looked like, objectively, through the author of John. Without an understanding of this historical world, the text may be interpreted incorrectly or its meaning may elude us (Thiselton 2009: 23). Theologically speaking, if acknowledged at all, to know the intention of the author is to know the intention of God across time and space. This, of course, creates the perception that the scholar and teacher hold the key to the text's meaning.

In keeping with this tradition, but not with the same underlying assumptions of how to come to an understanding, this chapter on the historical background of John (who, where, when, why, and how John was written) begins with similar questions. Like those before me, I also aim to understand the rootedness of John but with a different goal: to thematize the process of discovering this rootedness. I am not interested in studying the historical background of John for the sake of some core meaning behind the intent, such as "what happened"; rather, I am concerned with exploring how one reaches some understanding of John's historical background. More specifically, by studying the historical background of John, I am not interested in knowing John better than others before me, thus trying to dismiss them as scholars and henceforth giving me some scholarly authority, but rather to understand John differently by examining the historical process that interpreters (including myself) employ in reaching a semblance of John's historical background. In a conversational way, I shall ask John questions, but John will also ask me questions, particularly about my identity and ideological commitments in the process of such a historical reconstruction. When one can engage difference respectfully and honestly, the opportunity to know the other (John, in this case) is that much more possible.

Before proceeding, a word about the theology of John is in order. This volume is not a delineation of John's theology, although it will engage some theological themes such as dualism, belief, and community (ecclesiology). The volume is more along the lines of an ideological engagement with John, with a focus on the way meaning (through the interaction between text and reader) serves to create and/or sustain relations of domination and liberation. The latter aim of liberation would be my theological commitment. While there are many studies that focus on the theology of John, this volume chooses to focus briefly on some traditional questions (such as the historical background of John) as well as literary questions, but pursuing both through an ideological approach. Focusing on some historical questions allows me to make this volume accessible to those who are quite interested in the relationship between "what happened" and "that which is said to have happened." This volume begins with a discussion of who John was, when and where John was written, and why John was written. The task aims not to capture the vision of John but rather to understand how, among many narrativizations of history about John, I (and the tradition) reached various conclusions about the historical background of John.

The Historical Identity of John: Fixed and/or Fluid

Many views about the identity of John exist in the tradition of Johannine scholarship. What many of the views have in common is that the historical identity of John—at the end of the day—is fixed, fixed in the sense that someone or more than one someone composed John somewhere during some time for some reason. I prefer to think of the historical identity of John as both fixed (as stated above) and fluid—fluid in the sense that the identity is constantly changing, depending on who (i.e., the interpreter) is doing the identification. For this chapter's purposes, I am interested in that part of the continuum where fixity is located.

An interpreter determines the fixity of John's historical identity based on scientific probability, namely, what "evidence" out there outweighs other evidence that secures John's historical identity as historical fact (or how things really were). As with any historical reconstruction, "the standards for, and of, objectivity are" based on the present's historical fabric (Palmer 1969: 65). And the historical fabric at the time of the rise of modern historical criticism in biblical studies (nineteenth century) is concurrent with the rise of scientific history in general (Appleby, Hunt, and Jacob 1994: 52–90). Thus, the standard employed in naming the identity of "John" is based on a notion of history governed by the hermeneutical principle of reason that is scientifically influenced, with objectivity and positivism as the guiding principles. The emphasis on scientific reasoning is seen in the historical reconstruction of John's identity. In what follows, I present four views on or four possibilities about the identity of "John" as the author. As mentioned, the identity of "John" is fixed if "identity" is viewed as something singular. For this interpreter, "John's" identity is multiple, but also always becoming—a principle reflective of my own adoption of a fluid identity. Subjectivities shift constantly as people privilege certain histories over others. Likewise, in reconstructing "John" the author's identities, scholars do so by privileging certain parts of "John's" history and identity over others.

Below I look at four historical factors that help identify who, where, when, why, and how John was written: authorship, provenance, date, purpose, and compositional history.

Authorship

Early church tradition, namely, Irenaeus of Lyons (125–202 CE) around 180 CE, presents one of the earliest suggestions that the author of John or the Fourth Gospel is John the son of Zebedee, an apostle named in the list of the apostles in the Synoptic Gospels (Mk 3:14-19, Mt. 10:1-4, and Lk. 6:13-16). Irenaeus also believed that this John was the Beloved Disciple mentioned in the Gospel of John (13:23-24; 20:2-10; 21:2, 7, 20-24) who also served as an eyewitness (1:14; 19:35; 21:24-25) (Irenaeus, *Against Heresies* 3.1.1, cited in Culpepper 1998: 33).

This tradition is supported by Eusebius, who received it from Irenaeus, who received it from Polycarp, an apostle of John (Eusebius, *Eccl. Hist.* 5.20.5-6, cited in Culpepper 1998: 33). Thus, the tradition of John as one of the apostles of Jesus (known as the son of Zebedee in Matthew, Mark, and Luke and the Beloved Disciple in John) is based on historical retrieval of surviving sources. The reconstructive tradition also aims to create a direct line of tradition ("rule of faith") from John to Polycarp to Irenaeus, thus silencing any other tradition at the time (e.g., Gnostic Christians) that would break this line of tradition. In essence, the various identities reflected in the internal evidence of the Gospels are elided or infused to emerge as John, an apostle (son of Zebedee) who also happens to be the Beloved Disciple and eyewitness in the Gospel of John.

However, this dominant tradition is not without questions. First, John the son of Zebedee is only mentioned in Mk 3:17 and Mt. 2:10. Luke 6:14 only mentions that John was an apostle like the other apostles named. Is this the same "John"? Second, the Beloved Disciple who is mentioned in the Fourth Gospel is thought to be the eyewitness to the Jesus event and the one who wrote about this event (19:35; 21:24). However, these texts do not say explicitly that the Beloved Disciple is the eyewitness or the one who wrote the Fourth Gospel; it is only inferred based on the narrative context: 19:35 ("He who saw this has testified so that you also may believe. His testimony is true, and he knows that he tells the truth") and 21:24 ("This is the disciple who is testifying these things and has written them, and we know that his testimony is true"). Thus, the former text (19:35) does not mention directly who "he" is, and the latter text (21:24) only says that the eyewitness spoke the truth. Hence, is the eyewitness the Beloved Disciple? Is the author of the Fourth Gospel the Beloved Disciple? Is the eyewitness and the author even the same person, given that the first plural pronoun "we" (21:24) appears to differentiate the author from the one who is narrating the event? Third, some have suggested that the unnamed disciple mentioned in Jn (1:40) is the Beloved Disciple, but again this is not mentioned directly. Fourth, some scholars have pointed to the author of the Fourth Gospel as the author of the Johannine epistles (1, 2, 3 John). However, the Gospel and the epistles never mention this shared identity, neither explicitly nor implicitly. This tradition comes from Eusebius once more (*Church History* 3.39.4, cited in Gundry 2003: 257). Finally, some have linked the author of Revelation who does identify himself as John (Rev. 1:9), but, among other things, there is no direct evidence that this is the "John" who authored the Fourth Gospel. Thus, the reconstruction of the identity of John is based on reasonable inference by comparing texts and tradition with other sources. And sources, as mentioned in the introduction, are not neutral. Using the process of eliminating unlikely possibilities leads many to believe that the only reasonable identity for the author of the Fourth Gospel is John, an apostle (son of Zebedee) who is mysteriously also the Beloved Disciple. However, some Johannine scholars today would argue that the author of John is not a single identifiable person but rather a symbolic representative of a school of thinking like an ancient school of philosophy, where John was studied, composed, and put together by incorporating different sources and points of view (Culpepper 1975). At the end, what we really have are narratives, based on a poverty of sources that are repositioned by scholars to create new narratives about who John was.

All of this repositioning is driven by the principle that if we could know the author of John we can know the meaning of the Fourth Gospel, and, theologically speaking (unconsciously or consciously), know the mind of God. This aim goes as far back as the early church theologians (e.g., John Chrysostom) and continues today. Nonetheless, I am less concerned with the definitive identity of the author and more interested in how a conclusion is reached. Understanding the routes scholars take to reach a fixed identity of John helps to understand why certain scholars read the Fourth Gospel the way they do. I am also less concerned with the intent of the author as tradition and interpreters have stated or argued, and more interested in how John affects readers—hence my selection of an ideological approach. Consequently, I am more resigned to say that the author is fluid, not because one cannot piece together reasonably a truthful picture of "John" but because fluidity allows for more options to exist regarding the historical identity of "John" without intentionally highlighting certain pieces of the author's identity over others. Finally, the process of discovering the author of John suggests that interpreters are engaged in myth-making—as I do at times in the classroom. They contribute in taking a dearth of contradictory ancient evidence and modifying it or cleaning it up to attach it to history for ecclesial and public consumption. In reality, the author of John is made in their image—as I have done by seeing John's identity as fixed and fluid.

Provenance

Where was the Fourth Gospel written? Accompanying the goal of situating John within its historical rootedness in order to better understand its origins—and hence its meaning—is the question of where John was composed. Such questioning of John's provenance assumes that its location is recoverable. In other words, the closer one reads or reaches back into history to recover a piece of John's background, the closer one gets to learning about its provenance. In such a quest, the aim is to try to accumulate both internal evidence (within the text) and external evidence (outside the text) to better approximate where John was written. If I know where you are from, I can better understand what you are trying to say. The same principle applies to texts. If I know where John was written, I can better understand John.

Ephesus is the location where tradition situates John. Once again, Irenaeus, in *Against Heresies* (3.1.1, cited in Culpepper 1998: 33), states, while identifying John, the disciple of Jesus, that John wrote the Gospel when he was staying in Ephesus (Asia Minor). Thus, many scholars think Ephesus was the place of composition because they assume the author of John and that of Revelation is the same person—Revelation was thought to be written in Patmos (Rev. 1:9), an island off Ephesus. One problem with Ephesus as the site of composition is that when Ignatius wrote to the Christian community in Ephesus in the early second century (around 110 CE), he made no mention of Jesus's disciples having been there. Another problem with Ephesus is that it is not supported by strong external sources. More importantly, no internal information in John points to Ephesus as the location. There are some who still approach John with the position that Ephesus was the location but use Ephesus as a rhetorical, heuristic tool to try to make sense of John's negotiations with the Roman imperial world (Carter 2008: 14). In this way, Ephesus is not seen in isolation from the wider imperial world. Ephesus remains the spot where John was composed even as a rhetorical tool, with a repositioning of sources to examine such evidence within an imperial framework of the Roman Empire. However, like all choices, it excludes other possible locations. To be fair, following the rules of the academic guild, writing a simple one-sided historical narrative of the past is not what interpreters are trained to do, even though many historical reconstructions result in one-sided narratives. I disavow simple one-sided historical narratives and seek to attend to and offer other possibilities. For instance, John's introduction of the Logos (1:1-18) suggests a Hellenistic context overall. John's anti-Jewish rhetoric suggests a large Jewish presence where John was written (perhaps Syria). And John's independent and maverick characteristic as a Gospel suggests a location far removed from other Christian communities (perhaps Alexandria). Overall, Ephesus is still retained by many who hold onto the tradition and even support it with Acts 18-19, where Ephesus is mentioned as a place where there are various expressions of Christianity mentioned (18:24-26), where John's disciples are mentioned (19:1-7), and where Christianity is seen as superior to Judaism (19:11-16). All of these occurrences are reflected in John's Gospel (Powell 1998: 126). But again, choosing from available sources and assembling them into a narrative of provenance, the making of Ephesus is complete.

With historical reconstruction, it is vital to gather as much evidence as possible to support a position. With the question of provenance, the evidence is just not there to point to a definite place. Nonetheless, the aim for some, following the rules of historical reconstruction outlined by the academic guild, is to imagine John to have been written from Ephesus. Such a move is a hermeneutical tactic in order to understand John from the perspective of its location or the place of the original audience. The process, not without merit, aims to establish an empathetic relationship with the original historical audience from their location or to put oneself in the position where the author was composing. The process by which interpreters move from tradition (Ephesus as the place of composition) to where it is "confirmed" to have been written (Ephesus) makes the question of location worthy of increased attention. By making John an object of modern learned discourse where context plays a role in understanding, this move also tells readers (repeatedly through textbooks) how to read John and what John meant for its day and time (Carter 2008: 3–18).

Date

The same historical approach is employed to determine when John was written. Again, the assumption behind this historical inquiry regarding the dating of John is that truth exists in history. By careful accumulation of information (internal or external), comparison, and simple deduction, the dating of John or any text for that matter will reveal itself to the closest possible temporal approximation of its final composition. The date of John's final composition is approximately established around 90–135 CE. The earlier date, 90 CE, is based on information found inside John (internal evidence). Textbooks, especially introductions, based their conjectures on three passages in John: 9:22, 12:42, and 16:2. In each of these three passages, a reference that "the Jews" would put believers of Jesus out of the synagogue (*aposynagōgos*) becomes part of the supporting evidence. Many believe that this expulsion took place after the Romans destroyed the Jewish temple in 70 CE, thus causing an identity crisis among the Jewish community regarding who belonged and who did not. Hence, many Christian interpreters came to believe that Jesus-believers or Jewish Christians were expelled from the Jewish community. Such theory of expulsion is also supposedly supported by an event. A council of Jews convened in Jamnia (The Academy at Jamnia, 90 CE) determined who was included in and excluded from the Jewish community. In other words, those who did not identify as "Jewish" (based on Jamnia's definition) were expelled. As a result, some Jewish groups had to make a decision if they were going to remain on the side of the Jamnia council (Jewish) or follow the believers of Jesus ("Jewish Christians"). In sum, these three passages that highlight the expulsion from the synagogue around the time of this Jamnia event led scholars to approximate John's date around 90 CE, allowing time for this situation regarding Jewish identity to make its way into the Johannine story.

The later date, 135 CE, is based on papyri evidence (external evidence). In the early part of the twentieth century a papyrus fragment named P52 was discovered and scholars dated it to approximately 135 CE. On P52 was Jn 18:30-31, which is the earliest piece of extant New Testament manuscript. If John was circulating around 135 CE, then John must have been written prior to 135 CE. Thus, 90–135 CE is the time period that scholars work with to establish the period when John was composed.

Opinions do fluctuate within the temporal range based on how scholars assemble and interpret the internal and external evidence. Some scholars lean toward a date prior to 90 CE and some even date the Gospel prior to 70 CE (since Jn 5:14 infers that the temple, which was destroyed in 70 CE, is still standing). Some also lean closer toward the 90 CE end of the temporal range (or even earlier) based on those texts in John that point to a lower Christology or a theology that does not appear to have developed (by Western standards of development), and some lean closer to 100 CE or afterward because of passages in John that imply a more developed or higher Christology. These kinds of thinking are surely based on the assumption that history develops the same way across times and places. The West's understanding of history and epistemology is key to deciding "what happened."

Based on modern historical standards, it is actually reasonable to target a time period such as 90–135 CE for John's composition, given how challenging it is to reconstruct this period so distant from the present and with very little historical information. However, it is an approximation that scholars are proposing and one that requires a critical reflection on how the dating, just as we did with authorship and provenance, is determined. A brief look at the historical background of John—that is, the tradition of what most scholars narrate is the historical background of John—shows that we are no closer to knowing the past. In fact, I would argue that scholars know more about the now (present), particularly how they create a narrative of John's historical background (authorship, provenance, date) that fits into an epistemological world of possibilities for Western readers. An example of this "fit" is found with the purpose of the Gospel of John.

Purpose

Why was John written? To access John's purpose for writing, interpreters aim to capture the lived experience of the intended audience or what is known as the *Sitz im Leben* of a text or Gospel. So, for whom was the Gospel written? Interpreters often go straight to Jn 20:31: "But these are written that you *may come to believe* that Jesus is the Messiah, the Son of God, and that through believing you may have life in his name" (my translation and my emphasis). However, based on the Greek, I can also translate Jn 20:31 as, "But these are written that you *may continue to believe* that Jesus is the Messiah, the Son of God, and that by believing you may have life in his name." The question is which translation comes closest to the "original" and thus reveals its purpose. If one chooses the first translation, which translates the verb *pisteuō* ("to believe") as an aorist active subjunctive (*pisteusēte*) and hence "may come to believe," it suggests that the Gospel is intended for nonbelievers, so that they might be brought to believe or to have faith. But if one chooses the second translation, which translates the verb *pisteuō* ("to believe") as a present active subjective (*pisteuēte*)—notice the absence of the sigma or "s" in the Greek word—the translation suggests that the Gospel is intended for believers, so that they might continue to believe or stay in their faith. Both Greek words (*pisteusēte* and *pisteuēte*) are supported by respectable ancient Greek documents. The first, *pisteusēte* ("may come to believe"), is based on some authoritative and early copies of John and the New Testament (e.g., Sinaiticus [fourth century CE] and Alexandrinus [fifth century CE]), while the second, *pisteuēte* ("may continue to believe"), is based, for example, on an important fragment of a papyrus of John (P66) dated to be around the third century CE. Both Greek words have other ancient supporting documents, but these are some very important ones. The point here is that ultimately interpreters choose a translation that involves an interpretive selection of evidence and differential ranking of ancient manuscripts, following the rules of the academic guild that are based on what is called textual criticism and translation theory. Most importantly, these rules convey authority and establish credibility; they (as used by the interpreters) determine the narrative of John's textual and translation history. Thus, is the purpose of John written to nonbelievers to be brought to faith in Jesus or to believers to remain in their faith, or both?

Another step in determining the purpose of John is to understand the redaction history of John's composition. What interpreters aim to do is to turn to the identity of the Johannine community as well as its relationship to other communities represented in the Gospel. These other communities include the Samaritans and Gentiles (4:1-42; 10:16, 12:20-22); their addition in John suggests, for some, that John was also composed for the purpose of bringing these groups to faith in Jesus. Another community is made up of the followers of John the Baptist (1:29-34; 3:30), thus to some extent it is thought that the author of John mentions them to assure readers that Jesus, not John the Baptist, is the Son of God. As a similar corrective measure, the purpose of John in part was also to correct any thinking or misunderstanding that Peter, rather than the Beloved Disciple, is the model disciple to be emulated (13:23-25; 18:17, 25-27; 19:26-27; 20:1-10; 21:7). For many interpreters, understanding how and why certain groups were added in John's narrative contributes to understanding why John was written. If they were not important, they would not have been included. Of course, editors (as well as narrators) also include (or narrate) only what is important to them, thus perhaps silencing other participants (and reasons) that garnered the composition (or the storytelling) of John.

It should be noted that these three possibilities (incorporating other communities; correcting any misunderstanding about John the Baptist; presenting the Beloved Disciple as the model disciple) for John's composition have not gathered the same attention as the hypothesis that John was written due to the expulsion of Jewish Jesus-believers from the synagogue. As mentioned above, the dominant hypothesis is based on a few texts: (1) 9:22 and 9:34 suggest that the blind man is expelled from the synagogue because of his belief in Jesus; (2) 12:42 intimates that others are afraid to confess Jesus lest they too be expelled; and (3) 16:1-4 insinuates that Jesus, speaking to the disciples, predicts that they will also be expelled. All three "expulsion" texts lead to the conclusion that John was written for the Jesus-believers who were expelled from the synagogue because of their faith in Jesus—that they "may continue to believe" in Jesus. In other words, John was written to strengthen the faith of Jewish Jesus-believers who were experiencing a traumatic identity crisis because of hostilities against them or an intrafamilial dispute among Jews (Reinhartz 1998: 111–38).

J. Louis Martyn argues for this "expulsion" hypothesis in *History and Theology in the Fourth Gospel*. He aims to confirm this proposition with historical information outside the Gospel of John. Martyn examines the period toward the end of the first century (80–90 CE) when the Pharisees at the Yavneh Academy were attempting to consolidate Judaism under their authority. These Pharisees, in order to consolidate Judaism, introduced a benediction against heretics (*Birkat ha-Minim*) to the synagogue prayers. Part of the prayer said: "for the renegades let there be no hope … and let the Nazarenes and the heretics perish as in a moment and be blotted out from the book of life, and with the righteous may they not be inscribed" (Jocz 1979: 51–7, cited in Brant 2011: 166). Martyn believes that this prayer against heretics (i.e., Jewish Jesus-believers) was aimed at dissenters of Judaism who became the nascent Johannine community.

If true, the conflict between the synagogue leaders and Jewish Jesus-believers centered around two identity issues concerning Jesus: (1) Was Jesus the Messiah? This question is behind 9:22 when those who were put out of the synagogue were those who confessed Jesus as the Christ; and (2) Is Jesus God? This question is reflected in other places in John when it was interpreted that Jesus was, in a blasphemous act to the Jewish community, making himself equal to God (e.g., 5:18; 8:58-59; 10:33).

With these two possible concerns behind the expulsion hypothesis, Martyn proposes that John be read on two levels. One level is the story of Jesus situated in the early decades of the first century CE and the other level is the story of the Johannine community (or church for some) near the end of the first century CE. Martyn believed that the early hearers of the Gospel also would have heard/read in accordance with this two-level drama approach.

As I suggested above, such reasoning about why John was written is based on a hypothesis. It is a hypothesis that has had a major impact on how John has been read and is read today. It is also a powerful hypothesis that is reproduced in textbooks (not to mention sermons), which are prime resources in facilitating people's understanding of early Christian beginnings (Lozada 2013: 151–64). It is a hypothesis that attributes the reason for the writing of John to two opposing communities (Jewish synagogue versus Jewish Jesus-believers), thus creating a meta-narrative of the beginnings of Johannine community (as well as Christianity)—a meta-narrative that portrays the Jewish synagogue negatively and the Jewish Jesus-believers positively. In other words, the Jewish synagogue kicked out Jewish Jesus-believers; they played the identity gatekeepers, so to speak. Such a narrative script (re)presents the Jewish synagogue for sure as the instigators. As I have argued earlier, representation influences behavior, which in this case has influenced not only how Judaism is treated today by anti-Semitic groups but also how other religious communities with different beliefs systems other than Christianity, such as Islam, are treated.

Adele Reinhartz proposes a different and arguably more persuasive hypothesis to explain the division reflected in John between Judaism and Jewish Jesus-believers (Reinhartz 1998: 111–38). Reinhartz reexamines the data presented by J. Louis Martyn and points out that, based on the exegesis of the Johannine text and the employment of the two-level approach to reading John, scholars tend to read and accept Martyn's hypothesis as if it applies to the entire Gospel's social setting (*Sitz im Leben*) as well as the historical experience of the Johannine community. But what if one were to examine these three "expulsion texts" with other texts in the Gospel, such as with the story of Mary and Martha in 11:1-44 and the story of Lazarus in 12:1-11? How would Martyn's expulsion theory read then?

In the story of Mary and Martha (11:1-44), the narrative points out that Jewish people, who do not have a prior belief in Jesus as Messiah, comfort Jesus-believers (11:19) on account of Lazarus's death—Lazarus was a believer himself. Such a reading questions the assumption about the "expulsion" texts that the Jews of the synagogue expelled Jewish Jesus-believers because of their belief in Jesus. If the Jews did expel Jesus-believers from the community, then why does the narrative talk about Jewish non-believers mourning for Lazarus and even comforting the family? Furthermore, in 12:11, the Jewish authorities do express concern that some Jews are leaving on account of their faith in Jesus, but their concern does not lead them to expel these new believers; rather, the new believers leave of their own volition. If this is the case, the story that "the Jews" of the synagogue forced Johannine Jesus-believers out of the synagogue is questionable.

Reinhartz builds on this argument further by positing the lack of external evidence that the Jewish synagogue indeed expelled the Jewish Jesus-believers. She points to other texts that show that it is possible, for example, that (1) the Jewish Jesus-believers did confess their belief in Jesus and at the same time showed their allegiance to the Jewish synagogue; and (2) the Gospel was possibly written not directly related to the historical situation of the expulsion but rather as an expression of their faith (20:30-31).

All of this is to say that, according to Reinhartz, the meta-narrative that the Jews of the synagogue expelled Jewish Jesus-believers or Jewish "Christians" is not as tightly put together as Martyn has presented it. Her alternative reading of the Jewish Jesus-believers points to a community within a complex social situation where self-identity is in process rather than a community responding to being expelled. Such alternative reading does not posit the Jewish synagogue and the Jewish identity in John in a negative light; instead, it reads the Jewish Jesus-believers in the process of self-identification in the midst of various historical, social, theological, and ideological issues in the world behind the text.

What Reinhartz does is to provide an alternative historical narrative of the social conditions behind the text of John. Such a reappraisal of the expulsion theory does not necessarily lead to a better understanding of John but simply a different one, and one that brings other voices out as part of the Johannine narrative.

Compositional History

Finally, related to Martyn's expulsion hypothesis is John's compositional history. The hypothesis serves as a means to better understand the various literary stages that gave rise to John as well as the various communities represented in John. The compositional history that remains axiomatic for Johannine interpreters and represented in textbooks (which represents an institutionalization of history) comes from Raymond Brown's *The Community of the Beloved.*

The hypothesis is that John was composed along five stages of development. The compositional hypothesis is based on a notion of history that can be known and can make sense of the past. It is also an employment of history that sees time as real, universal, and sequential. Interpreters working with this notion of history are capable of labeling historical epochs, people, and texts in terms of development. In other words, all development is measured in terms of progress against the Western world's development and notion of time, with the West serving as the norm and constituting the most advanced development of all societies (Appleby, Hunt, and Jacob 1994: 52–3). John's five stages of development work with such a notion of history.

The first stage of development of John is reflected in 1:35-41. This stage included an original group of Palestinian Jews, including followers of John the Baptist who held some views reflected in the Dead Sea Scrolls (e.g., dualism of light and darkness). This group also had a traditional view of the Messiah (so a low/human Christology) as one who would descend from David and work miracles like Moses or Elijah. This group supposedly collected synoptic-like sayings and miracle stories, with the latter becoming the Signs Source—a source that presents the signs or miracles in the Gospel of John (2:1-12; 4:46-54; 5:1-9; 6:1-13; 9:1-7; 11:1-44; 21:1-8; some scholars include also 6:15-25). This group included former followers of the Baptist (perhaps) and the Beloved Disciple. This first stage, along with the second stage to follow, was a stage prior to the writing of the Gospel (thus a timeframe of mid-50s to late 80s CE).

The second stage of development is reflected in Jn 4:4-42—the story of the Samaritan woman. The assumption at play here is that Jewish Jesus-believers who opposed the temple carried out a mission to bring Samaritans to their community. As a result, these Jewish Jesus-believers, influenced by Samaritan ideas—especially the idea that their Messiah is to be the new Moses and called the "savior of the world" (4:42)—accepted the Samaritans as part of the Johannine community. The acceptance of the Samaritans, now believers, led to a high/divine understanding of the Messiah (e.g., "savior of the world"). Such a new understanding of Jesus compelled the Jews of the synagogue to expel the Johannine "Christians," for such an understanding made Jesus equal to God (cf. 5:18). The leader of this group of the second stage is assumed to be the Beloved Disciple.

The third and fourth stages are the period when the Gospel was put together or composed. Brown estimates that this took place around 90 CE. The third stage can be gleaned from 12:20-23 and 12:37-42, that is, when the Greeks come to Jesus. This is the period when the Gentiles were included within the Johannine community, thus leading to a more universalistic outlook. This is also the stage when the Johannine Christians migrated from Palestine to the regions of Ephesus of Asia Minor or some other city in Syria (7:35) to prepare to compose the Gospel.

The fourth stage is when John was written. Brown identifies seven groups during this stage. The first three were outsiders who encountered conflict with the Johannine Christians: (a) the world (9:39; 12:31, 35-36); (b) "the Jews," especially the chief priests, scribes, and the Pharisees; and (c) those continuing to follow John the Baptist (3:22-26). The second three are considered sympathizers: (a) Jews who secretly believe in Jesus, but fear being expelled from the synagogue (e.g., Nicodemus in 3:1-21); (b) Christians whose faith is inadequate (6:60-66; 7:3-5; 8:31; 10:12); and (c) believing Christians of other communities led by Peter, who is portrayed as competing with the Beloved Disciple (6:60-69; 21:20-23). Finally, the last group is the collective of Johannine Christians themselves.

It is not until the fifth stage, after the composition of the Gospel and the writings of the Epistles (100 CE), that Jn 21, Jn 1:1-18 (the prologue), and Jn 7:53-8:11 were added to the Gospel.

Overall, the hypothesis that John was composed along five stages of development becomes the standard narrative among Johannine interpreters. What does get overlooked in studying this hypothesis is the assumption of history that undergirds it. When history and science combine to explain the world event in the mid-nineteenth century, historians like Brown in the twentieth century will view the world behind the text as knowable and "scientifically" retrievable. What is problematic with such an understanding of history, among other things, is that history is assumed to mean the same thing for all cultures and times—again, something knowable and "scientifically" retrievable. However, history means different things to different cultures (Kwok 1995; Dube 2000). Brown assumes that all history is understood the same way across time and places. The development of John as a text makes sense to the majority (though not all) of Western readers who see meaning as something that is knowable and "scientifically" retrievable in history. As mentioned, Brown, like many Johannine interpreters, is simply using the rules of doing historical retrieval that were created and continues to be supported by the academic guild out of the Western world. In a sense, most if not all scholars trained in the Western world, including myself, follow these rules and practices.

In conclusion, trying to reconstruct the historical background of John—whether it is its authorship, provenance, date, purpose, and compositional history—says more about those doing the reconstruction than about John's historical context. Interpreters know the past no clearer than they know the present. It is therefore especially important that we understand the historical process in which they are engaged: namely, how they move from asking, "what happened" to declaring, "that which is said to have happened." I will try to show this when I address the identity of "the Jews" in Chapter 3. The issue of doing history is not simply about trying to recover "what happened," it is also understanding the process of "that which is said to have happened." Reinhartz aims to get at this process by trying to lift up those voices that have been silenced by Martyn and others. This is the value of an ideological approach to John: one can see that power comes into play with the choices one makes in accumulating the so-called evidence and narrating that evidence as history.

References

Appleby, J., L. Hunt and Margaret Jacob (1994), *Telling the Truth about History*, New York: W. W. Norton.

Brown, R. E. (1979), *The Community of the Beloved Disciple*, New York: Paulist Press.

Bryant, J. A. (2011), *John*, Grand Rapids, MI: Baker.

Carter, W. (2008), *John and Empire: Initial Explorations*, New York: T&T Clark.

Culpepper, R. A. (1975), *The Johannine School*, SBL Dissertation Series, 26, Missoula: Scholars.

Culpepper, R. A. (1998), *The Gospel and Letters of John*, Nashville, TN: Abingdon.

Dube, M. W. (2000), *Postcolonial Feminist Interpretation of the Bible*, St. Louis: Chalice Press.

Gundry, R. H. (2003), *A Survey of the New Testament*, 4th ed., Grand Rapids, MI: Zondervan.

Kowk, Pui-lan. (1995), *Discovering the Bible in the Non-Biblical World*, Maryknoll, NY: Orbis Books.

Lozada Jr., F. (2013), "Teaching the New Testament," in Francisco Lozada Jr. and Greg Carey (eds.), *Soundings in Cultural Criticism: Perspectives and Methods in Culture, Power, and Identity in the New Testament*, 151–64, Minneapolis, MN: Fortress Press.

Lozada Jr., F., and T. Thatcher (eds.) (2006), *New Currents through John: A Global Perspective*, Atlanta: Society of Biblical Literature.

Palmer, R. E. (1969), *Hermeneutics: Interpretation Theory in Schleiermacher, Dilthey, Heidegger, and Gadamer*, Evanston, IL: Northwestern University Press.

Powell, M. A. (1998), *The Gospels*, Minneapolis, MN: Fortress Press.

Reinhartz, A. (1998), "The Johannine Community and Its Jewish Neighbors," in Fernando F. Segovia (ed.), *"What Is John?" Volume II, Literary and Social Readings of the Fourth Gospel*, 111–38, Atlanta: Society of Biblical Literature.

Thiselton, A. C. (2009). *Hermeneutics: An Introduction*, Grand Rapids, MI: Eerdmans.

Further Reading

Ashton, J. A. (1991), *Understanding the Fourth Gospel*, Oxford: Clarendon Press.

Brown, R. E. (1966–70), *The Gospel According to John*, 2 vols., Anchor Bible 29-29A, New York: Doubleday.

Brown, S., and C. W. Skinner (eds.) (2017), *Johannine Ethics: The Moral World of the Gospel and Epistle of John*, Minneapolis, MN: Fortress Press.

Bultmann, R. (1971), *The Gospel of John: A Commentary*, trans. G. R. Beasley-Murray, R. W. N. Hoare, and J. K. Riches, Philadelphia, PA: Westminster.

Callahan, A. D. (2007), "John," in B. K. Blount (ed.), *True to Our Native Land: An African American New Testament Commentary*, 186–212, Minneapolis, MN: Fortress.

Hengel, M. (1990), *The Johannine Question*, trans. J. Bowden, Philadelphia, PA: Trinity Press International.

Keener, C. S. (2003), *The Gospel of John: A Commentary*, 2 vols., Peabody, MA: Hendrickson.

Köstenberger, A. J. (2004), *John*, BECNT, Grand Rapids, MI: Baker.

Kysar, R. (2007), *John: The Maverick Gospel*, 3rd ed., Louisville, KY: Westminster John Knox Press.

Liew, T.-S. B. (2002), "Ambiguous Admittance: Consent and Descent in John's Community of 'Upward' Mobility," in M. W. Dube and J. L. Staley (eds.), *John and Postcolonialism: Travel, Space and Power*, The Bible and Postcolonialism, 7, 193–224, Sheffield: Sheffield Academic Press.

Lozada Jr., F., and T. Thatcher (eds.) (2006), *New Currents through John: A Global Perspective*, Atlanta: Society of Biblical Literature.

Martyn, J. L. (1979), *History and Theology in the Fourth Gospel*, 2nd ed., Nashville, TN: Abingdon Press.

O'Day, G. (1995), "The Gospel of John," in L. Keck (ed.), *New Interpreter's Bible*, vol. 9, 491–865, Nashville, TN: Abingdon Press.

Reinhartz, A. (1994), "The Gospel of John," in E. S. Fiorenza (ed.), *Searching the Scriptures*, vol. II, 561–634, New York: Crossroad.

Schnackenburg, R. (1968–82), *The Gospel According to St. John*, 3 vols., trans K. Symth, New York: Seabury.

Segovia, F. F. (ed.) (1996), *"What Is John?" Readers and Readings of the Fourth Gospel*, Symposium Series 3, Atlanta: Scholars Press.

Segovia, F. F. (ed.) (1998), *"What Is John?" Volume II, Literary and Social Readings of the Fourth Gospel*, Atlanta: Society of Biblical Literature.

Smith, D. M. (1999), *John*, Abingdon New Testament Commentaries, Nashville, TN: Abingdon Press.

Thatcher, T. (2006), *Why John Wrote a Gospel: Jesus–Memory–History*, Louisville, KY: Westminster John Knox Press.

2

John's Literary Background: Plot

Chapter Outline

Narrative of Unsettlement (1:1-18) 32
Narrative of Travel/Crossing (1:19–17:26) 35
Narrative of Resettlement (18:1–21:25) 49
References 53
Further Reading 54

In the previous chapter, I focused on John's historical background (authorship, provenance, date, purpose, and compositional history) as both fixed and fluid: someone, somewhere, at some time, in a particular way wrote John for various reasons. However, the past is always written from the present, so John's historical background is influenced by the selection of sources and how the interpreter positions them to generate a new narrative about this history. The past (what happened) functions together with the present (that which is said to have happened), thus projecting an historical reading of John that is constantly changing. Such a principle continues when Johannine interpreters, like myself, employ literary criticism (or narrative criticism). The final form of a literary document—now with a particular genre, discourse, narrative events and settings, and characterization—is the result of someone's selection and decision to tell a story (what happened) through her or his interpretation of John's narrative (that which is said to have happened). A major difference between an historical approach and a literary approach is that the latter is interested not in the pretextual history of John but instead in the narrativization of John, that is, the story that is advanced in the text of John itself. In what follows, I will focus on the plot of John. The plot opens the doors toward understanding other literary aspects of John.

With all literary readings of plot, certain literary aspects—just like historical sources for historical background—are highlighted over others. In this particular reading of the plot, two literary aspects are thematized. First, the structure of the plot is ordered by the motif of journey; and, second, the causality of the plot is guided by the dualistic (two parts of a larger whole) literary motif of recognition and nonrecognition. These two literary aspects (journey and recognition/nonrecognition) not only are reflected in the plot of John as part of John's literary design but are also results of a selective reading of John's narrative.

Both these literary aspects, journey and recognition/nonrecognition, have been chosen and emphasized by other Johannine literary scholars in their readings of the plot of John (see Culpepper 1983; Segovia 1991). Other scholars have chosen to focus on the genre of the Gospel as an ancient biography or drama (e.g., Stibbe 1992; Talbert 1992; Bryant 2011), on a specific sequence of events (e.g., geographical settings, Jewish festivals, signs), or on particular relationship between events throughout the plot (e.g., a conflict between belief and unbelief as responses to Jesus, between two realities [world above versus world below], or between empire and Jesus as God's commissioned agent) (e.g., Kysar 1984; Segovia 2007; Carter 2008). What all these scholars do have in common is a concern for the unity or coherence of the plot that often involves attempts to delimit the plot's shape in various ways, such as a U-shaped structure with the plot moving downward and gradually moving upward (descent toward ascent), or from a stable condition of events (Jn 1-4) toward instability (Jn 5-19) and back toward stability (Jn 20-21) (Resseguie 2001). They are also interested in understanding the affective power of John's plot or its desired response from its readers, whether they are implied readers or flesh-and-blood readers (e.g., Moloney 1993, 1996, 1998; Reinhartz 2001). I agree with many Johannine literary interpreters that it is important to understand not only the genre at play in studying the plot but also those factors that play a role in the development of the story, such as sequence, causality, unity, and affective power. Like these Johannine literary scholars, I also shall engage these literary factors in making sense of John's plot.

To begin, I understand the genre of John as an ancient biography, centered on the life of a holy man, who is on a journey—a mythic journey of descent–ascent (Segovia 1991). Such a journey is understood to entail a move of unsettlement toward a movement of resettlement by Jesus. Such an overall movement is presented along three particular movements: a narrative of unsettlement (1:1-18), a narrative of travel/crossing (1:19–17:26), and a narrative of resettlement (18:1–21:25) (Lozada 2017). Of course, this holy man is Jesus the Son of God, who descends from the world above to this world and returns to the world above. The main travel/crossing journey (1:19–17:26) is guided by an underlying conflict of recognition and nonrecognition of Jesus as the Son of God and is structured around four journey cycles. The first three follow a pattern of Jesus traveling to Galilee, followed by a corresponding journey to the city of Jerusalem: a first Galilee/Jerusalem journey (1:19–3:36); a second Galilee/Jerusalem journey (4:1–5:47); and a third Galilee/Jerusalem journey (6:1–10:42). Both Galilee and Jerusalem serve as destination points for each journey cycle, with Jesus traveling through Bethany (1:28, 36); the countryside of Judea (3:22); Samaria (4:3-4), with a brief stay in Capernaum (2:12). The fourth and final journey is to Jerusalem (11:1–17:26), with a passing through Bethany (11:1) and a final appearance in Galilee (21:1) (Segovia 1991). The narrative of unsettlement or prologue (1:1-18) summarizes these journeys, and the final narrative of resettlement or return traces Jesus's journey back to the world above (18:1–21:25), still guided by recognition and nonrecognition scenes. To be sure, this recognition/nonrecognition motif has its roots in ancient drama and follows a dualistic system of opposites (recognition or nonrecognition of Jesus as the Son of God) for the most part (Culpepper 1998: 72). As you will see, recognition of Jesus is not always clear-cut; in the stories, some characters' recognition involves ambiguity (Hylen 2009). Consequently, the motif of recognition and nonrecognition functions as two ends of a continuum, with characters who encounter the Johannine Jesus vacillating along the continuum or leaning toward one end or the other. Thus, as Jesus freely travels and crosses borders (metaphorically and physically), his words and actions call on characters to recognize or not recognize (or vacillating between the two) him as the Revealer, Son of God, Christ. The motif recurs throughout the plot, also calling on flesh-and-blood readers to make a decision on Jesus's identity.

This chapter will also bring in an ideological perspective to the plot. First, a contemporary notion of recognition is brought to bear on the plot. In the ancient world, recognition suggests discovery of identity—a character (recognizer) of another character's true identity (recognized), thus influencing their relationship (affection or enmity) as well as their fate

(Culpepper 1998: 72–7). This fundamental pattern is also found in John. However, in the postmodern world, whereas recognition may also function this way, it could also suggest a broader understanding where claims for recognition of ethnic/racial, sexuality, gender, and religious differences, for example, call for social equality. This understanding is called a politics of recognition—visibility and respect over invisibility and disrespect in society. It is a resistant movement—if you will—against assimilation to the dominant or majority way of life or identity. In short, it calls for a reciprocal relation between subjects in which each subject sees the other and respects the other. By recognizing the other, the other becomes a subject; by not recognizing the other, the other is rendered invisible. Thus, differences of subjects are not abolished, but rather valued and celebrated (Fraser and Honneth 2003: 7–33).

This understanding of recognition foregrounds the following reading of the plot of John. On the one hand, my reading of the plot of John assumes the ancient understanding of recognition, played out through the conflict of belief or unbelief in Jesus; on the other hand, a broader understanding of recognition plays a role in seeing that the plot has the effect of an assimilating drive: it moves or entices a reader to adhere to the dominant point of view of the plot, thus leaving no room for difference to be treated with equality or respect. What you have at the end of the plot is basically an in-group community versus an out-group community: a duality or an either/or choice between recognition and nonrecognition, with little concern for the effect such recognition might have on the other (Tan 2006). What follows is, again, simply one reading of the plot of John, informed by the ancient motif of recognition and the present-day understanding of recognition.

Narrative of Unsettlement (1:1-18)

John begins with a cosmic narrative of unsettlement (1:1-18). This narrative division revolves around three important narrative units (1:1-2; 1:3-17; 1:18) aimed to both distinguish the identity of the Word (Jesus) and to reveal the Word's mission to the world. A closer read of this narrative will be presented in Chapter 4, with a slightly different focus on ideological representation.

With the first unit (1:1-2), the Word begins in the world above, the cosmos. This cosmic setting above is where the narrator explains the Word's identity in relationship to God: "In the beginning was the Word, and the Word was with God, and the Word was God" (1:1). In these three independent clauses, the narrator points out that the Word's relationship to God is defined temporally ("in the beginning"), physically ("with God"), and theologically ("is God"). Without a doubt, the question of identity is well placed in the forefront of this Gospel from the very beginning. What is learned is that the Word is not just eternal, but the Word is also the authoritative Word of God; that is, the Word is God's expression of God's self to humanity, and the Word's origin is surely in the world above. This point of view is clearly established in the very first verse, which shows an image of the Word (Logos) at the top: "He was in the beginning with God" (1:2).

Drawing the point of view away from the world above, the second unit (1:3-17) turns toward the world below. The narrator does so with a focus on the Word, draws attention to the Word coming into the world, and delineates the Word's mission and response to the mission by the world. Thus, the revealing of the Word's identity and mission begins when the Word is characterized, first, as coming into the light and life and, second, as one engaged in a battle that results in success (1:3-5). Such reporting provides an indication about the results of the Word's unsettlement from the world above. A dualistic or binary battle between light and darkness shall occur, with the light overcoming and mastering (*katelaben*) the darkness. Thus, the Word's mission will encounter hostility in a world full of conflicts between belief and unbelief or recognition and nonrecognition (including partial recognition by some).

The Word is further identified by way of the narrator's introduction of John the Baptist (who provides testimony about the Word coming into the world) and of the Word's mission to bring light (faith or belief) to all of humanity (1:6-9). The cause of unsettlement is further revealed; it has to do with the Word's mission to bring faith to the world of unbelievers (1:7). What is more, this introduction of John the Baptist is significant, for without him, Jesus is left with no human witness. The witnessing of the Word (light) by comparing John the Baptist to the light ("he [John] was not the light," 1:8a) conveys the point of view that John's identity and mission is not equal to the Word's. He simply serves as witness to or an ally of the light. Together, they challenge any misrecognition of the Word.

The narrator then turns to the Word's mission (1:10-13). This is a mission that will encompass one of conflict: unbelief in the Word leads to nonrecognition, belief in the Word to recognition. A duality or binary is again repeated: a world of belief and a world of unbelief. As this narrative continues to unfold, the Word is presented as the authoritative and powerful one, establishing a cultural order between worlds and eliciting successful recognition from those who believe (children of God) and misrecognition from those who do not believe (not children of God). This foreshadowing of the hardening lines between believers and unbelievers implies separation and even hostilities with unbelievers and adversaries working against Jesus and his believers.

In this dualistic order of things, the Word is God's emissary in the flesh (1:14-17). The Word becomes human, the one who travels freely from the world above to the world below. The Word is crowned with grace and truth signifying the Word's special authoritative identity. This commanding identity is again confirmed with the narrator asserting a clear difference between John the Baptist and the Word in flesh—Jesus Christ (1:17). Thus, the narrator prepares the readers to pick sides: either recognize or do not recognize the Word, without reflecting on the effects toward others (i.e., the unbelievers).

This leads us to the final unit (1:18) of the narrative with the Word returning to the world above (cosmos). Once more, the special relationship between the Word—now the Son—and the Father is highlighted in terms of intimacy. Thus, the narrator conveys a viewpoint regarding the Son's authoritative position in both the world above and the world below, providing a place-based story with certain groups (unbelievers) belonging to a certain fixed place (a world below).

Overall, the narrative of unsettlement introduces the identity and mission of the Word (Jesus) in an authoritative way as the Son of God. The reason for unsettlement has to do with the Word's mission in the world below. The Word departs from the world above to bring light and life to the unbelievers, and the Word takes on flesh so that those who believe may become children of God for eternity. As a result, the Word's mission will entail freedom of movement that will lead to encounters that will cause some to recognize him/the Word as Jesus or not recognize him at all. At the end, the Word/Jesus will return to his origins, next to God who calls for belief in one identity and one allegiance, thus drawing definitive lines or borders between believers and unbelievers. For sure, the Word or Jesus freely moves between worlds and peoples, but the narrative of unsettlement represents a movement with the causal impact of reinforcing divisions between "us" and "them." All will be called to adopt one identity in Jesus as Christ and one allegiance (or "citizenship") as a child of God, thus ironically reflecting an imperial–colonial arrangement in which the identity of believers and unbelievers reflects and manifests the identity of the world above and world below. Such a reflection suggests a dualistic world, purging anything with a different "way of life" or identity (Segovia 2007; Carter 2008).

Narrative of Travel/Crossing (1:19–17:26)

The second major division in the plot of the Fourth Gospel is organized into four journey cycles (Segovia 1991). Recognition scenes are narrated throughout these journeys, leading to successful and unsuccessful (as well as ambiguous or developing) recognition scenes and, at the same time, creating a dualistic reality between the world above and the world below. As the plot unfolds, this duality rejects any broad understanding of recognition where distinctive perspectives (e.g., different belief systems) are accepted.

The First Galilee/Jerusalem Cycle (1:19–3:36)

The first Galilee/Jerusalem cycle (1:19–3:36) consists of several recognition scenes (or narrative sections) that leave characters either recognizing Jesus or not; as mentioned above, some characters are ambivalent in their recognition. The journey begins in Bethany, continues to Galilee, and then crosses into Jerusalem and ends in the surrounding area of Judea (3:22).

The point of view in this first journey cycle is to see Jesus as the Savior, pulling characters (and flesh-and-blood readers) toward this single affiliation or calling on characters (and readers) to take sides. This first cycle involves three narrative moves: (1) a discussion of Jesus's identity through John the Baptist in Bethany (1:19-34); (2) the journey toward Galilee (1:35–2:12) and then Jerusalem (2:13-31); and (3) finally a return to Judea with a discussion of John the Baptist in the countryside (3:22-36).

Toward Galilee: This division begins with John the Baptist in Bethany beyond the Jordan (1:19-34). John, as mentioned in the narrative of beginnings (1:6), serves as a witness to the identity of the Word/Jesus. John initiates Jesus's public ministry by bearing witness to Jesus before the religious leaders sent by "the Jews" or the Pharisees to question him (1:19, 24). These leaders want John to identify himself, since he is baptizing or gathering a group of followers, but John provides a negative confession and denies that he is the Christ (1:20, 24). However, on the next day, John recognizes Jesus as the "Lamb of God" who takes away the sin of the world—a title that invokes the context of Passover and the idea of sacrifice (1:29). Such witnessing by John reveals that John is fully aware that Jesus is superior (in rank) to him (1:30). He knows because he has seen the Spirit descend on Jesus and remain on him, thus conferring God's confirmation (1:32-34). This recognition scene is crowned with the announcement by John that Jesus is the Son of God (1:34). As John recedes from this scene, Jesus comes to the fore. This view of Jesus as the Christ, the Lamb of God, and the Son of God confirms his identity as the one who takes away the sin of the world. This true identity of Jesus will now confront other characters throughout the cycle and plot.

While still in Bethany, John publicly introduces Jesus as the "Lamb of God" (1:36) to two of John's disciples (an unnamed disciple and Andrew); after hearing John, the disciples recognize Jesus as the Son of God. They want to know where Jesus is staying, for they want to be part of his following. In a sense, they commit themselves to Jesus and follow him both physically and philosophically; they become part of his in-group or community. They also address Jesus as "Rabbi" ("teacher"), a title that points to Jesus's identity as an important religious leader. This title, "Rabbi," along with the other titles ("Lamb of God," "Son of God," and "Christ"), are all confirmed when Andrew finds his brother, Simon (Peter), and refers to Jesus as the "Messiah," the "Christ" (1:41). It is Andrew who finds Simon first and then brings him to Jesus; in so doing, their action of coming to Jesus confirms their recognition in Jesus as the Messiah, the Christ. Their faith prompts Jesus to rename Simon as Cephas (which is Aramaic) or Peter—a name by which he will be forever known. To rename Simon as Cephas (Peter), Jesus is in effect showing his power. In other words, it is not, perhaps, Simon Peter who finds Jesus, it is Jesus who finds Simon Peter. Jesus is the protagonist who needs to be recognized. In effect, all of the disciples (Andrew, the unnamed disciple, and Peter) are called to suspend their particular way of life and identity to follow Jesus and to take on a new way of life and identity as believers in Christ.

On the next day, Jesus, with the three disciples, travels to and reaches Galilee (a two-day journey from Bethany, cf. 2:1) when Jesus recognizes the identity of two other soon-to-be disciples (Philip and Nathanael, 1:43-51). While the first three disciples sought out Jesus, Jesus takes the initiative and calls Philip to be another one of his disciples (1:43). Like Andrew seeking out Peter, Philip seeks out Nathanael to tell him that he has found "Jesus son of Joseph from Nazareth" (1:45). Nathanael, a true Israelite, at first is a bit unconvinced of Jesus's identity, for he is skeptical that Jesus could come from Nazareth, thus suggesting that Nazareth is an unimportant place. In other words, Jesus's origin is questioned, so Nathanael goes to see Jesus himself; when he does—after Jesus manifests his identity by knowing where Nathanael was before (omniscience)—Nathanael is convinced and recognizes Jesus's identity and thus commits himself to follow him. He even calls Jesus "Son of God, King of Israel" (1:48-49).

Thus, all five disciples recognize the identity of Jesus (as "Lamb of God," "Son of God," "Rabbi," "Messiah" or "Christ," "the one whom Moses wrote about," "King of Israel," and "Son of Man"—all titles attached to Jesus's identity in this recognition scene (1:35-51)) and thus give up their former way of life and identity (they are now believers in Jesus) to follow Jesus. From the beginning, as seen in the narrative of unsettlement (1:1-18), the story of the Word/Jesus is one about recognition. By recognizing Jesus, the disciples are committed to follow him. They recognize that he is not some ordinary man, but rather the Son of Man, who is from the world above, travels below to share his life with the world below, and will eventually return to the world above (1:50-51).

On the following day, in Cana (in the area of Galilee), Jesus performs the first of seven signs/miracles: the changing of water into wine at a wedding (2:1-12). This sign confirms Jesus's creative power in the world below. In the context of identity and recognition, Jesus is surely recognized by his mother, who calls on him to perform a miracle. Before the wedding is over, the wine has run out; his mother calls on her son, Jesus, presumably to replenish the wine so that all those present can continue to fill their cups with wine. In this particular scene, Jesus is not seeking recognition per se. He is not ready to do anything, but his mother does want him to help out. She pushes Jesus into public ministry, but Jesus reminds her that his hour has not arrived or that God's plan for him has not started. Nonetheless, Jesus changes water into the best wine and fulfills both his mother's wishes and, more importantly, God's plans for him. Jesus draws public recognition through the act of the miracle. This act points to Jesus's identity once again as creator (1:3, 14). By manifesting God's glory (1:11), this act conveys the point of view that Jesus represents the world above of light and life, as opposed to the world below of darkness and death (1:4-5). Jesus's miraculous act demonstrates to his disciples his true identity as the Son of God. They recognize him as the Christ and thus continue to follow him, along with others, on his journey (2:12). Slowly, an in-group community continues to grow with defining lines marked around them.

Toward Jerusalem: The first journey to Galilee then moves on to Jerusalem (2:13–3:21). This is his first trip to Jerusalem in the story and it is during the feast of Passover (2:13). The recognition scene takes place at the temple (2:15), where Jesus initiates an aggressive clash with the moneychangers who make the temple a house of trade and thus keep it from being a true house of God (2:16). As a result of this conflict, "the Jews" question Jesus and ask for a sign to show them what authority supports his actions (2:18), since the priests have authority over the rituals of the temple. Jesus has already established his unique relationship with the Father by calling the temple his "Father's house," thus pointing to his identity as the Son of God (2:16). In lieu of a sign, Jesus answers "the Jews" with a request to destroy the temple and in three days he would raise it up (2:19). The ambiguous statement leads "the Jews" to take Jesus's statement literally. But actually, with the help of the narrator stepping in, Jesus, as we learn, is really referring to his own suffering, death, and resurrection later in the story. This prediction will lead many to recognize and believe in him (1:23). The narrator never indicates whether "the Jews" who questioned Jesus are believers or not. Their line of questioning appears to be simply an inquiry (Hylen 2009: 28). Thus, it is unclear what results from this scene in terms of recognizing Jesus's identity by "the Jews." The narrator does state that the disciples would remember this event and that their faith would be deepened. In this sense, the scene does function to lead to full recognition for and by believers.

This ambiguity in relationship to Jesus's identity is also reflected in the following recognition scene. Jesus encounters Nicodemus, a Pharisee, who struggles to recognize the identity of Jesus (3:1-21). Nicodemus, a leader or ruler of "the Jews," comes at night—perhaps suggesting he could not speak to Jesus by day—and calls Jesus, "Rabbi" (3:1-2). Nicodemus, through his actions and words, knows that Jesus comes from God because the power of God is with Jesus. In other words, Nicodemus recognizes Jesus as one who can do signs through God; however, to what extent does he recognize Jesus's full identity is uncertain.

Jesus, instead of a talk about signs, speaks to Nicodemus of a new birth to enter the Kingdom of God. Following a pattern of misunderstanding, Nicodemus understands this new birth or born anew as a second physical birth, which to him is not possible. Jesus aims to clarify what he means: it is not physical birth that Jesus is speaking about; rather, one must be born anew of water and the Spirit to be a member of the Kingdom of God. Jesus explains this position with a further teaching on the Spirit, but Nicodemus remains confused (3:8-9), so Jesus resorts to a brief discourse on the Son of Man with the hope that Nicodemus, a teacher of Israel, will understand his identity and his mission (3:10-15). His discourse culminates with a précis—if you will—of his discourse. Jesus conveys that he, God's only Son, is a gift from God (3:16). Because of God's love for the (unbelieving) world, God offers God's Son so that whoever recognizes or believes in him will not be condemned but rather receive eternal life. God not only offers the Son, the Son is sent by God to offer salvation to the world (3:17). All of this is to teach Nicodemus, although he fades away in the narrative, of Jesus's identity as the Son of God and his mission to bring salvation to the unbelieving world below. For sure, Nicodemus's confusion or misunderstanding of how one is born anew/above or born of the Spirit (3:3, 8) initiates a vacillation of recognition, leading Jesus to address such uncertainty. Like other characters in John, Nicodemus is portrayed as being in a process of "formation"—he goes back and forth with regard to his recognition of Jesus. He is an example, perhaps, of one who lives between two worlds or "ways of life" or identities.

The first Galilee/Jerusalem cycle comes to an end in 3:32-36. Those who recognize Jesus's identity as the Son of God are rewarded with eternal life and those who do not will perish. These are the two ends of the continuum or duality, but, as seen through Nicodemus, there are those who are conflicted and will move back and forth the continuum until they can reach a state of recognition or nonrecognition. At the same time, the plot's attempt to reduce recognition to a final binary, "either/or" response suggests that identity as expressed through the text is reduced to a single, definitive dimension in the story world. This is an imperialistic expression of identity (Carter 2008).

Consequently, the first Galilee/Jerusalem cycle (1:19–3:36) demonstrates successful, unsuccessful, and ambiguous recognition encounters. Believers in Jesus as the Son of God/Word choose to follow him and those who do not believe continue to challenge him. Those in between are struggling to recognize. Such scenes of discovery have the resultant effect of creating two worlds: a world of belief and a world of unbelief, and those in the former receive the gift of eternal life and those in the latter receive condemnation. Thus, recognition as a motif plays a central role in the construction of these groups as opposites: an in-group community against an out-group community.

The Second Galilee/Jerusalem Cycle (4:1–5:47)

Toward Galilee: From Jerusalem, Jesus journeys toward Galilee, with a transitory stop through Samaria (4:1-54). Before he arrives in Galilee, he engages a Samaritan woman at Jacob's well. The Samaritan woman surely represents difference in terms of ethnic/religious and gender identity. Jesus initiates a conversation with her—through several exchanges, some involving misunderstanding on the part of the Samaritan woman—that eventually draws her to recognize Jesus. The misunderstanding begins when Jesus requests a drink of water at a well from the Samaritan woman, who does not recognize him at this point in the story. The narrator makes it a point to state that "Jews" do not have dealings with Samaritans; this statement functions perhaps to explain why she would not know who Jesus is (4:9). It is not until Jesus moves the conversation toward his identity that she comes to recognize Jesus.

Jesus, after requesting a drink and as a response to her hesitation of who he is, explains to the Samaritan woman that only if she had known that it was Jesus who was speaking to her and that he had something to offer her, she would know to give him a drink, and Jesus in return would have given her "living water" (4:10). However, like Nicodemus, the Samaritan woman misunderstands the allusion to "living water." She thinks it is some magical water that will keep her from thirst, but "living water" (4:15) points to Jesus's identity as the eternal source of life for those who recognize him. She remains confused, so Jesus, as he did in demonstrating his knowledge of Nathanael's past (1:47-48), exhibits knowledge of the Samaritan woman's sexual past (4:16-18). Such knowledge leads the Samaritan woman to recognize Jesus as a prophet and, consequently, brings her faith to her community, which also comes to believe in Jesus (4:39-42). In due course, the community itself encounters Jesus directly, thus confirming the Samaritan woman's experience of recognition. At the end, the community bestows Jesus with the title "Savior of the World" (4:42).

Jesus then crosses back into Cana in Galilee, where he performs another sign: healing a royal official's ill son in Capernaum (4:43-54). Rather than a discourse to explain who he is as he did with the Samaritan woman, Jesus uses a sign to speak to his identity. The royal official, who was apart and distant from his ill son who is presumably at the point of death, appeals to Jesus for a healing. The official's faith in Jesus directs Jesus to command the official to go home where he will find his son healed. Interestingly, there is really no sign like the changing of water into wine; the official's simple recognition of Jesus as the source of life leads to his son's healing. The recognition of Jesus as the one truly sent from God leads the official and his household to a deeper recognition of Jesus as the Son of God.

Toward Jerusalem: Traveling to Jerusalem the second time (5:1-47), Jesus encounters a lame man who is unable to reach a pool (Bethsaida) to seek its healing powers (5:1-9b). Jesus knows that this man has been there trying to reach the pool for many years, so Jesus asks him whether he wishes to be made well. The man responds ambiguously with neither a definite yes nor no. Instead, he responds by saying why it is difficult for him to reach this pool. Nonetheless, Jesus heals the man instantly. However, the day of the healing is the Sabbath and, "the Jews" make a point to remind the man, according to the law, it is not lawful to work on the Sabbath (5:9c). "The Jews" thus want to know who healed the lame man, yet the lame man does not know. It is only when Jesus finds the man in the temple that Jesus's identity is recognized and disclosed to "the Jews." Such recognition, however, is not exactly a full recognition; it is perhaps a partial recognition, but it is not exactly a full recognition that leads to faith per se (at least not in a way that John's point of view finds adequate). It only discloses Jesus's identity as the lame man's healer to Jesus's adversaries, "the Jews," who consequently threaten Jesus's life with death (5:18). In response to this warning, Jesus engages in a long discourse (5:19-47) to defend or legitimize his identity. This "legal" recognition defense is an attempt to persuade "the Jews" and other nonbelievers of his true identity as the Son of God; "the Jews" find this, however, difficult to accept (5:18).

The second Galilee/Jerusalem cycle continues the recognition motif of Jesus with the help of various characters. In this cycle, the lame man appears to vacillate on the continuum of recognition but eventually reaches a partial recognition (since he appears to disclose Jesus's identity to his adversaries), while other characters lean toward the end of the continuum of full recognition (the Samaritan woman and the royal official) or the end of nonrecognition ("the Jews"). These various recognition scenes in this second Galilee/Jerusalem cycle show Jesus traveling and crossing various borders—both physically and metaphorically. In so doing, he encounters not only different characters but also difference; he calls on them all to recognize him. Through these encounters, lines are being drawn to create an in-group and an out-group community. The in-group will receive eternal life, while the out-group will perish. The challenging aspect of these recognition scenes is that—from the point of view of the story—Jesus, as a character, does not reciprocally recognize characters whom he encounters, unless they recognize him as the Son of God. In other words, if they do not recognize Jesus, they will be seen as the personification of evil and, collectively, as a group to be feared and shunned. Recognition scenes motivate characters to act in welcoming ways, but they can also lead characters to be perceived as a threat to a "normative" way of life if they do not believe (5:18).

The Third Galilee/Jerusalem Journey Cycle (6:1–10:42)

The third Galilee/Jerusalem journey cycle begins with Jesus retreating across the Jordan to avoid the hostility coming from "the Jews" (5:18). This journey takes place during the second feast of Passover in John's Gospel (6:1–10:42). This cycle consists of numerous recognition scenes, reflecting a politics of recognition with Jesus at its center.

Toward Galilee: John 5 ends with Jesus in Jerusalem. He then travels to Galilee and crosses to the other side of the Sea of Galilee. The narrator opens with a large crowd following Jesus during the feast of the Passover. They are in essence attracted to Jesus as a source of life because of the many signs he has performed on the sick (6:1-2). Moved by the crowd's following, Jesus decides to sit down on top of a mountain from nearby Bethsaida (cf. 1:44); he turns to Philip and asks him how might provisions be bought to feed the large crowd. Of course, as the narrator says, Jesus asks Philip to test him, for Jesus has already decided to feed the crowd. In other words, Jesus examines Philip to see if Philip recognizes him as the source of life. After estimating that they do not have enough funds to feed the large crowd, Andrew, Simon Peter's brother, brings a lad or poor boy who has five barley loaves and two fish. Working with little food, Jesus performs another miracle by multiplying the food for the many—five thousand are present (6:10). Thus, Jesus responds to the disciples' perception of futility with a feeding for the large crowd. The response by the crowd is interesting. At first, this feeding by Jesus seems to represent a successful recognition scene, since many in the crowd want to crown him king (6:14-15); yet the encounter is actually a failed recognition scene, since the crowd wants to crown him king by force—thus implying that they do not really understand who he is and what his mission is about. In other words, they experienced the sign and decide to associate Jesus with the anticipated prophet they have been waiting for, but Jesus is not ready. In John, Jesus controls his hour (6:15; cf. 2:4).

Yet, through this sign of feeding, Jesus does confirm his identity. After he escapes the crowd's intent on making him king, Jesus miraculously walks across a stormy sea to Capernaum (another crossing), with the disciples following in a boat. Jesus approaches the frightened disciples in their boat and reassures them that he is the one: "It is I" or "I am" (6:20). Such expression, given its similarity to God's response to Moses's question in Exod. 3:14, reveals his true nature: he is God. In the remainder of the chapter, Jesus expands on this true identity. We see that he is one who is above nature (6:16-21) and one who is the eternal bread of life (6:22-65). With both of these narrative events, Jesus contrasts his teachings with the crowd's understanding. Their view or recognition of Jesus is ambivalent. Like the Samaritan woman who wanted to continue to quench her thirst, they want food to continue to feed their stomachs, but they understand food in a physical way rather than a spiritual way. It is not until they call Jesus "Lord" that they recognize that Jesus is speaking about food in spiritual terms or as eternal life (6:33-35). To be sure, Jesus is "the bread of life"; he confirms this statement with his other "I am" statements (6:41, 48, and 51; cf. 6:35; 8:12; 9:5; 10:7, 9, 11, 14; 11:25; 14:6; 15:1, 5). However, while some are coming to recognize Jesus, others such as "the Jews" continue to question his true identity (6:41-52). Jesus responds by emphasizing that he (as Christ) became flesh and blood (fully human) so that he could bring life to those who believe (6:53-59). Such teaching, like it did for "the Jews," led his own disciples to question Jesus's true identity (6:60-61). The disciples were divided into two groups: believers and unbelievers (6:64). Simon Peter, taking the lead among and representing the believers and twelve disciples, confesses or recognizes Jesus as the Holy One of God (6:66-71).

All in all, the motif of recognition is surely at play in this important chapter regarding Jesus's identity. The crowd and the disciples are definitely vacillating on the continuum of recognition, while "the Jews" are surely on the end of nonrecognition. But they are not alone. There are some disciples who will fail to recognize Jesus and go their own way (6:66). For sure, Jesus remains the center in a politics of recognition.

Toward Jerusalem: John 7 begins with Jesus traveling about in Galilee and with his disciples pressing him to go to Judea (Jerusalem), since it was the season of the Festival of the Booths. More importantly, the disciples want Jesus to perform his work in public. However, like Jesus's mother who wanted Jesus to honor her requests, the disciples are also trying to persuade Jesus to honor theirs by going to Judea to carry on his ministry rather than yielding to God's will. Eventually Jesus does go to Jerusalem, but he goes privately or secretly (7:10). The disciples' push to go to Judea indicates again their misunderstanding of Jesus's true identity or at least the timing of his mission vis-à-vis the will of God (7:1-9).

In the following narrative within this third cycle (7:10–10:42), Jesus encounters hostile opposition. It intensifies during this trip to Jerusalem, with his opponents claiming that he has a demon within him (7:20) and sending police or officers to arrest him (7:32, 44); Jesus, in response, refers to them ("the Jews") as children of the devil (8:44). The entire cycle centers on Jesus's identity, and various characters are trying to discern who Jesus is; this leads to division among them (7:43). For sure, those in authority are not recognizing Jesus as the Christ, with the exception of Nicodemus who wants to provide a safe space for Jesus to be heard (7:51). These encounters show that recognition of Jesus's identity depends on whether characters believe that Jesus's source of authority comes from the world above or whether it comes from the world below. God who sent Jesus is the primary source of Jesus's authority from the world above, while his opponents see his source emanating from the world below.

After a brief narrative of a woman taken in adultery (7:53–8:11), which I shall discuss a bit more in the following chapter, Jesus continues his discourse on his identity with further claims that approximates him with God ("I am the light of the world," 8:12), thus infuriating his adversaries even more (8:12-59). He also defines his identity by place or location: "You are from below, I am from above; you are of this world, I am not of this world" (8:23). As a result, his opponents attempt to stone him (8:59).

Interestingly, those who are teachers fail to recognize Jesus, but those who are powerless do recognize Jesus. A good example of this is the healing of the blind man (9:1-41). Jesus has already healed on the Sabbath a lame man who recognizes Jesus but fails to act on it (5:9), and now he heals a blind man who does recognize Jesus fully (9:7). Whereas the blind man recognizes Jesus, the Pharisees or "the Jews" (9:13, 18), who question the blind man about who healed him, are portrayed as those who are willfully "blind" to Jesus's true identity (nonrecognition). This is an important text when it comes to Jesus's identity. The healing of the blind man's sight reinforces the understanding of Jesus as the light of the world (9:5). The healing portrays a Jesus who can physically heal a person, thus shining light on him as the Son of God. At the same time, his act aims to bring spiritual light to those such as the Pharisees and "the Jews." He shows them the world above but they choose to belong to the world below. At the end, the healing of the blind man brings the now once-blind man to faith or recognition of Jesus, and this man's expulsion by "the Jews" from the synagogue as one who no longer belongs to their community. For sure, such miracle elicits many reactions from neighbors, his parents, and "the Jews," but it is only the blind man—now able to see—who recognizes Jesus as the one sent from God (9:24-34). Thus the point of view of the story sees recognition as an either/or choice in a struggle over belief in Jesus as the Son of God.

This compassion for the blind man extends further when Jesus declares himself the Shepherd of all—at least to those who wish to recognize him (10:1-21). The Shepherd separates the sheep that recognize him apart from those who do not recognize/hear him—such as those who did not believe the blind man in the previous chapter. For sure, Jesus is reaffirming his true identity. He, the Johannine Jesus, portrays his opponents as unbelievers because they fail to recognize his voice. Those who fail to recognize his voice are thieves, bandits, hirelings, and wolves who will not follow him; they are hence deemed by John's Jesus as a kind of outlaws. "The Jews," who are not his sheep, are drawing closer to taking out Jesus through physical action. They make another attempt to arrest Jesus, but Jesus escapes across the Jordan to a place (Bethany) where many recognize who he is (10:42).

With this third Galilee/Jerusalem cycle (7:10–8:59; 9:1–10:42), the point of view of the text remains in support of the world of belief/above and those belonging to it. There is surely a heightening of violence in this third cycle. From the point of view of the narrative, "the Jews" and others take issue with Jesus aligning himself as God. The result is a threat of violence upon Jesus. There is no question that the issue of recognition leads to both violence and issues of belonging. As long as the point of view of the Gospel maintains a portrayal of Jesus and believers in an either/or construct, it will imprison them in a single or superior way: this believers-versus-nonbelievers construct has the effect of even pressing partial believers toward the nonbelieving end of the pole. The result is a reinforcement of an in-group-versus-out-group community mentality.

The Fourth and Final Journey to Jerusalem (11:1–17:26)

The fourth and final journey cycle (11:1–17:26) for Jesus begins in Bethany and ends in Jerusalem where Jesus's identity results in his death (19:17-37). But prior to his death, a number of recognition scenes take place.

Toward Bethany: The journey begins with Jesus heading to Bethany (east of Jerusalem, cf. 11:1–12:10), where he will bring to life a friend, Lazarus, at the request of both Martha and Mary, Lazarus's sisters (11:1-44). Martha's first words to Jesus illustrate her faith and recognition of Jesus as the source of life (11:21-22). She not only declares her faith but also expresses her confidence in his power to bring life from the dead. Martha even calls him "the Christ," "the Son of God," and "the one who comes into the world"

(11:27). The sisters address Jesus as "Lord" (11:28), and Mary even falls at Jesus's feet showing love and great admiration for him (11:32). Martha does show some doubt, not so much of who Jesus is, but in why the stone needs to be taken away (11:39). At the end, the raising of Lazarus leads to a successful recognition of Jesus's identity or reconfirmation of it by Martha and Mary— Jesus is the resurrection and the life (11:25) and whoever believes in him shall never die (11:26). The miracle also brings the Pharisees and chief priests (Sanhedrin) to a final decision to kill Jesus (11:53). However, from the viewpoint of the narrative, Jesus does this miracle in accordance to God's will to save humanity and not in accordance with the will of humans to save the nation (11:51-52).

Still in Bethany (11:55–12:11), Jesus is recognized once more through the large amount of perfume used by Mary to anoint his feet and signify his divine identity as the Son of God. Rather than pondering on the different identities of Jesus through titles and expressions, Mary through her actions demonstrates her recognition and belief in Jesus, foreshadowing even the day of his burial and resurrection (12:7). Thus, both scenes (Jesus's raising of Lazarus and Mary's anointing of Jesus) say something more about Jesus's identity: Jesus is more powerful than death itself. Jesus belongs to the world above where life exists, not in the world below where death exists.

Toward Jerusalem: The fourth journey to Jerusalem (12:12–17:26) begins with Jesus's final entry into Jerusalem (12:12-50). He enters Jerusalem in a triumphal procession for his final Passover (12:12-19), with many coming to see him. Jesus's raising of Lazarus leads some of the crowd to follow Jesus, but others still remained unconvinced of Jesus's identity (12:9-11). In a similar fashion, for sure, the Jewish authorities remain divided in their belief as to who Jesus is. Even the Greeks coming to Jerusalem to worship during the festival wish to see Jesus (12:20-26). Jesus's identity is not simply something that the Jewish people or Samaritans in the story are seeking to recognize; Greeks also wish to talk with Jesus. Jesus explains that his identity and mission involve also the Greeks. He is not simply in the world below for "the Jews," he is for all those who want to make a place for themselves in the world above. At the same time, Jesus's identity is also connected to death (12:27-36). To know him, one knows that it can lead to a violent confrontation. Jesus is aware of this so he goes into hiding. It is not yet his time; he needs time to prepare for his death (12:36).

Despite this disclosure by Jesus, those affiliated with the world below did not believe in him; however, there were some, including the Jewish authorities, who want to belong to the world above, yet they are afraid of being put out of the synagogue by the Pharisees (12:37-42). Jesus then makes another appeal to those who do not recognize him: he speaks as God commanded him to speak, so believe and they will receive the gift of eternal life (12:44-50). For whoever believes in the Word will live and those who do not are condemned. This universal appeal to many is asking them to make a decision on where they want to belong.

John 13:1-30 provides the beginning frame for the farewell scene in the Gospel (13:1–17:26). In a way, the farewell scene serves to reveal Jesus's identity further. It begins with Jesus washing the feet of his disciples (13:1-17)—the menial service generally performed by one of a lower social class—they understand him as one who serves others rather than being served (Lozada 2016). At the same time, Jesus reveals his identity as one who knows: he even knows who will betray him (13:18-30). Both notions of Jesus's identity, as one who serves and one who knows the mind of others, speak to his identity as one who desires recognition. It is a call for believers to go beyond the restrictions of their own social affiliations so they too can proclaim their own recognition of Jesus by following the example of their leader.

After revealing who the betrayer will be, Jesus focuses not only on his own identity but also on his imminent departure (13:31–17:26). Jesus speaks of his imminent death and resurrection as a glorification of himself and God. While God is glorified in Jesus, God will also glorify Jesus. After all of this is done, Jesus will return to the Father (13:31-32). Jesus will reiterate this theme of going away to the Father (14:3), but Jesus informs the remaining disciples that they cannot go with him—at least not yet. Instead, Jesus gives them a new commandment reminiscent of Lev. 19:18 and is repeated again in 15:12, 17: love one's neighbor as one's self. However, Peter is not satisfied, claiming that he does not understand why he cannot follow, showing that he still fails to completely understand Jesus's words and identity (13:36-38).

The disciples are concerned that they cannot follow Jesus, so Jesus provides words of comfort (14:1-14). The disciples should know that he is going away and will be with them for only a short time (13:33), but their recognition of Jesus continues to waver. He placates them by reassuring them that he will provide for them a place on their journey of recognition. Jesus will return to take them to his Father, but he reminds them that they already know the way to God. They have seen the truth in Jesus, who has made God known, and they have witnessed Jesus as life, for they have seen Jesus give the life of God—both physically and spiritually. Despite experiencing Jesus as the way, truth, and life, even Philip remains not quite sure. But Jesus is the invisible God made visible: to recognize Jesus is to know the Father. Jesus speaks, even using a double "amen" (14:12), to strengthen the disciples' belief in him and his identity. He even calls on them to pray and ask in his name.

Because of Jesus's love for his disciples and believers, he promises to send the Spirit (14:15-31). The Spirit is truth just as Jesus is the truth (14:6). To know the Spirit is to know Jesus and to know the Father, and to know the Father is to know Jesus and to know the Spirit. This unified identity is present in the believing community, yet the world of unbelievers below does not recognize the Spirit in Jesus, the disciples, or Jesus's words and works. For the believers, if they keep his commandments, they will remain with Jesus and God; there will be a mutual indwelling. They would obey and love Jesus and recognize him as someone who dwells in their lives. Thus, Jesus, at his impending departure, eases their discomfort, which is reflected in Judas's (not Iscariot) question of how Jesus will reveal himself (14:22). Jesus leaves them with peace as they prepare to encounter resistance from the ruler of the world.

Jesus also reveals his identity at this time as the true vine (15:1-17). This metaphor of the true vine emphasizes Jesus's relationship with the disciples and reveals not only the consequences for those who fail to believe but also the positive outcome for those who do. Jesus commands them to abide in him so joy will be in them and they will become friends going out into the hostile world and bringing Jesus's words of salvation to humanity. Jesus's words function to prevent them from leaving the believing community and to increase their faith in Jesus and the community (15:18–16:4a). His sending of the Spirit reflects his promise that he is inseparable from them if they believe (16:4b-15), yet they remain bewildered by asking Jesus where he is going. Still developing in their recognition of Jesus, they will take up Jesus's work and teaching after Jesus's departure.

The disciples' sorrow will soon turn to joy (16:16-24). Like a mother with a newborn child, they will turn from a state of anguish to one of joy. No one will be able to take such a joy away from a mother, just like no one will be able to take the joy away from the disciples when Jesus defeats the world. Jesus is preparing them for a new relationship, a new community. In this new relationship or community, Jesus wants them to offer prayers in his name. He assures them that their prayers will be answered because he has defeated the world (16:25-33). However, Jesus suggests that the disciples will not fully recognize Jesus in the coming events (16:32). As a way to continue this preparation for his departure and encouragement to deal with the world below, Jesus closes with a prayer to the Father and expresses his unity with God. This unity is articulated in Jesus interceding with God for himself (17:1-5), for his disciples (17:6-19), and for his believers (17:20-26), that they all may continue to be one in relationship to the unbelieving world.

Recognition again matters here. It allows the characters to form relationships with Jesus and to recognize themselves in relationship to Jesus. By following Jesus, they develop their recognition of Jesus as well as a different understanding of identity for themselves. The negative side of this is that while Jesus desires various characters to give recognition to him, Jesus is not always willing to recognize others, such as his adversaries, unless they change and believe. With the emphasis on recognition in this Gospel, hence, one becomes a subject only by recognizing Jesus. Otherwise, one lacks recognition (e.g., "the Jews") and is rendered invisible or condemned.

Narrative of Resettlement (18:1–21:25)

The final narrative concerns the betrayal, arrest, trial, death and burial, and the resurrection of Jesus. After the farewell discourse, the plot turns to emphasizing Jesus's lasting significance of calling on believers to believe. He will instruct the disciples to call on others to form a community in the world through which Jesus will manifest himself as God (Spirit).

Preparatory Events (18:1–19:16)

First, the arrest of Jesus by the ruling authorities (18:1-12) is marked by hostility (18:1-3). Note, however, how Jesus takes the initiative, comes to them (18:4), and asks them the same question he asked in the beginning of the Gospel: "Whom do you seek?" (18:4). Peter tries to interfere with Jesus's plan but he is quickly redirected to stand back and allow the arrest by those who represent the world (the soldiers, the captain, and officers of "the Jews") to happen (18:10-12). Second, after the arrest, the religious and political authorities take Jesus to Annas and Caiaphas to be questioned (18:13-27). While Jesus is defending himself before Annas and Caiaphas, Peter is recognized as one of Jesus's followers but he denies it three times. Peter lacks full confidence in his identity as a believer. Third, Jesus is taken to Pilate for further questioning (18:28–19:16). Similar to previous questioning, the focus is on Jesus's identity. Pilate is not concerned with Jesus's identity in terms of where he is physically from; he is more interested in whether Jesus is really the Son of God or not. Much maneuvering takes place between Jesus and Pilate but, in the end, it is Pilate who, under pressure, hands Jesus over to be crucified.

The Narrative of Death (19:17-42)

The death of Jesus begins with the crucifixion (19:17-37), followed by the burial (19:38-42). Jesus takes his own cross to be executed publicly between two unknown individuals at a place called in Hebrew "Golgotha," meaning "skull" (19:17). The title, "Jesus of Nazareth, King of the Jews," was ordered or caused by Pilate and placed on the cross (19:19). Jesus's name and crime were written in the national language (Hebrew), the official language (Latin), and the common language (Greek). Pilate wants the entire known world, from "his" (or John's) perspective, to know Jesus's name and crime (19:20). Present at the foot of the cross are four women (Jesus's mother; his mother's sister; Mary, the wife of Clopas; and Mary Magdalene) and the Beloved Disciple (19:25-26). Jesus's last words are "It is finished"; then he bows his head and dies, handing over his spirit. Jesus, through his death, surely becomes the one "who takes away the sins of the world" (see 1:29; 19:30). In closing, "the Jews" ask Pilate to take down the crucified bodies before the Sabbath, which also happens to be the Passover (19:31). Soldiers thrust a spear into Jesus's side to ensure death (19:31-34). The first part of the crucifixion of Jesus comes to a close with the narrator providing personal testimony to the event (19:35) and presenting these events as fulfillment of scripture (19:36-37, cf. Ex. 12:46; Num. 9:12; Zech. 12:10; 13:1. The second part involves Jesus's burial with the help of two secret believers, Joseph of Arimathea and Nicodemus (19:38-42).

The Resurrection Appearances (20:1–21:25)

The narration of Jesus's life finishes with four recognition scenes or resurrection appearances. Following the discovery of an empty tomb (20:1-10), Jesus appears to Mary Magdalene (20:11-31), then the disciples

(20:19-23), next to Thomas (20:24-29), and concludes with an appearance to the disciples once more (21:1-25).

After Jesus's body is prepared and laid in a tomb, Mary Magdalene comes on the first day of the week to the tomb and discovers it empty (20:1). She tells Simon Peter and the Beloved Disciple, and the two disciples run to the tomb and see not a body but only linen cloths where the body was lain—a sign that Jesus was not stolen but resurrected (20:3-5). Thus, both Simon Peter and the Beloved Disciple believe without seeing. The first part of this narrative section concludes with the two disciples returning home to confirm Mary Magdalene's earlier witness that the tomb is indeed empty (20:10).

The first appearance of Jesus is to Mary Magdalene. It is a significant recognition scene. When Mary returns to the tomb after discovering that Jesus's body has been taken away (20:11), she encounters Jesus but does not recognize him immediately (20:14). It is not until Jesus calls her by her name that Mary comes to full recognition and calls him "Rabboni" or "Rabbi" (20:16). She then goes to inform the disciples of what she has just witnessed (20:18). Jesus then appears to the disciples (20:19-23), who are hiding in fear of "the Jews," and greets them, saying, "Peace be with you" (20:19). Jesus then shows them "his hands and his side" to establish his identity; he is the same person who died on the cross. When the disciples express joy upon seeing him, Jesus greets them again with the same words ("Peace be with you") and says that he, now as the risen Lord, is sending them forth, just as he himself was sent by the Father (20:21). Jesus assures them that he will be with them through the gift of the Spirit and instructing them in their mission to the world (20:22-23). Next, Jesus appears to Thomas (20:24-29), who was not present in the previous appearance scene but who has already been known in the story as questioning (11:16; 14:5). This narrative with Thomas is also a clear recognition scene. But unlike the first two appearances of Jesus, Thomas is doubtful of Jesus's resurrection. He needs proof, so Jesus appears to Thomas and commands him to touch his resurrected body and urges him not to be faithless but to believe (20:27). Thomas confesses his faith with "My Lord and my God," thus making a dramatic change from doubt to belief or full recognition (20:28).

The first three resurrection appearances come to a close with a statement that many of Jesus's other signs are not written in "this book" (20:30). Those that have been included are written so that people may continue to believe (*pisteuete*) as well as so that some may begin to believe (*pisteusēte*) in Jesus as the Christ and the Son of God. The Gospel was therefore written to not only strengthen the faith of believers but also to lead unbelievers to faith in Jesus (20:31). Overall, these three recognition scenes end up as full recognition scenes. All of the characters are able to recognize Jesus and thus view their recognition as also their self-realization as believers.

The final resurrection appearance in John focuses on the disciples, with special attention to Peter and the Beloved Disciple (21:1-25). Jesus appears to the disciples in Galilee on the beach. Jesus gives them instructions on where to catch fish, but the disciples do not recognize him. Not until they catch a large quantity of fish does the Beloved Disciple recognize Jesus's identity and informs Peter (21:7). Jesus then invites them to eat and they do so with knowledge of his true identity (21:12). Jesus prepares the meal and serves the disciples with bread and fish (21:13). This recognition portrays an ideal reciprocal relationship between Jesus and his followers.

This last recognition scene (21:15-19) also reestablishes Simon Peter as a leading disciple. Jesus instructs Peter to feed his lambs and tend his sheep (21:15-17). The Gospel concludes with the narrator claiming authority as the one who wrote this Gospel (21:24) and with the statement that, given the vast amount of things that Jesus did, not all of the books in the world could have contained them (21:25; cf. 20:30-31).

Overall, the narrative of resettlement (18:1–21:25) narrates Jesus's return to the world above. Through this journey, the recognition scenes center on Jesus's identity and how the characters strive and finally manage to recognize Jesus. In this sense, these recognition scenes follow the ancient pattern of recognition. At the same time, recognition of Jesus as Son of God also, indirectly, constructs an either/or world. In so doing, the scenes, like all of the recognition scenes throughout the Gospel, create a dualist worldview where assimilation to the dominant point of view of the Gospel is a requirement for being accepted as a child of God.

In today's globalized and multicultural world where it is important to acknowledge and accept difference, recognition between persons should be reciprocal and equal. However, John's viewpoint promotes a recognition that is unidirectional and hierarchical. It is a standpoint that is out of sync, I believe, with the root impulse and telos of Christian faith itself. For John, Jesus, the hero, is to be recognized as such; otherwise, one is recognized as evil or portrayed in a negative light. What John's plot calls attention to is the complexity of recognition. Recognition, although understood ideally in a globalized or multicultural context as the necessary condition of being recognized by another subject without conditions, John's plot appears to lean toward a notion of recognition where the hero is always the hero and the other is always the other. John's notion of recognition calls on the characters (and readers) to be challenged by and changed from their encounter with Jesus, but also resistant to their encounter with "the Jews" and unbelievers.

References

Bryant, J. (2011), *John*, Grand Rapids, MI: Baker.

Carter, W. (2008), *John and Empire: Initial Explorations*, New York: T&T Clark.

Culpepper, R. A. (1983), *Anatomy of the Fourth Gospel: A Study in Literary Design*, Philadelphia, PA: Fortress Press.

Culpepper, R. A. (1998), *The Gospel and Letters of John*, Nashville, TN: Abingdon Press.

Fraser, N., and A. Honneth (2003), *Redistribution or Recognition? A Political-Philosophical Exchange*, London: Verso.

Hylen, S. E. (2009), *Imperfect Believers: Ambiguous Characters in the Gospel of John*, Louisville, KY: Westminster John Knox Press.

Kysar, R. (1984), *John's Story of Jesus*, Philadelphia, PA: Fortress Press.

Lozada Jr., F. (2016), "Narrative Identities of the Gospel of John," in D. N. Fewell (ed.), *The Oxford Handbook to Biblical Narrative*, 341–50, Oxford: Oxford University Press.

Lozada Jr., F. (2017), *Toward a Latino/a Biblical Interpretation*, Atlanta: SBL.

Moloney, Francis J. (1993), *Belief in the Word: Reading John 1–4*, Minneapolis, MN: Fortress Press.

Moloney, Francis J. (1996), *Signs and Shadows: Reading John 5–12*, Minneapolis, MN: Fortress Press.

Moloney, Francis J. (1998), *Glory Not Dishonor: Reading John 13–21*, Minneapolis, MN: Fortress Press.

Reinhartz, A. (2001), *Befriending the Beloved Disciple*, New York: Continuum.

Resseguie, J. L. (2001), *The Strange Gospel: Narrative Design & Point of View*, Leiden: Brill.

Segovia, F. F. (1991), "The Journey(s) of the Word: A Reading of the Plot of the Fourth Gospel," *Semeia* 53: 23–54.

Segovia F. F. (2007), "The Gospel of John," in F. F. Segovia and R. S. Sugirtharajah (eds.), *A Postcolonial Commentary on the New Testament Writings*, 156–93, New York: T&T Clark.

Stibbe, M. W. G. (1992), *John as Storyteller*, SNTSMS 73, Cambridge: Cambridge University Press.

Talbert, C. (1992), *Reading John, a Literary and Theological Commentary on the Fourth Gospel and the Johannine Epistles*. Reading the New Testament Series, New York: Crossroad.

Tan, Y.-h. (2006), "The Johannine Community: Caught in 'Two Worlds', in F. Lozada Jr., and T. Thatcher (eds.), *New Currents through John: A Global Perspective*, 167–79, Atlanta: Society of Biblical Literature.

Further Reading

Estes, D. (2008), *The Temporal Mechanics of the Fourth Gospel: A Theory of Hermeneutical Relativity in the Gospel of John*, Leiden: Brill.

Interpretation: A Journal of Bible and Theology (The Gospel of John) (October 1995), vol. XLIX (4): 341–89.

Painter, J., R. A. Culpepper, and F. F. Segovia (eds.) (2002), *Word, Theology, and Community in John*, St. Louis: Chalice Press.

3

John's Characterization: "The Jews," Women, and the World

Chapter Outline

"The Jews" 57
Women in the Gospel 61
The World 69
References 70
Further Reading 72

Another mode of entry into the literary dimensions of John is through characterization. As seen in the previous chapter, the characters in John, with the exception of Jesus and the portrayal of God, are round characters. What this means is that the characters are not one-dimensional, flat characters with static and unchanging identity, quality, or response. Instead, the characters are multidimensional, round characters with dynamic and evolving identity, development, or responses. They function in many different ways in the Gospel and respond to Jesus on a continuum: on one end, they believe in Jesus (e.g., disciples, women, the blind man) and, on the other end, they do not believe in Jesus (e.g., "the Jews," the world, and certain followers who did not believe, cf. 3:22-26; 6:66). Some scholars do not see these as clear-cut characters with unambiguous location or placement on the spectrum of belief or continuum of recognition. Instead, the characters represent ambiguity—constantly fluctuating in their responses to Jesus or degree of complexity in their characterization (Hylen 2009; Bennema 2013). Some also say that the characters cannot be understood in isolation from other characters, particularly along gender lines. To understand the female characters, one has to understand them in relation to male characters and Jesus as well as vice versa (Conway 1999).

For sure, scholars are not all in agreement in their interpretations of the characters. Some of these interpretations do employ a historical approach, in the sense that characters are read as representing various historical groups in the emerging Johannine community (or church). Other scholars, as seen above, employ a literary approach to better understand how characters (individuals or groups) function in one's understanding of John's story of Jesus. And some scholars draw on ancient characterization and rhetorical techniques to better understand Johannine characterization (Myers 2012).

In the following reading of various characters, I will draw on the work of previous scholarship to present an ideological perspective on character analysis.

An ideological perspective focuses on what ways the characters are represented, that is, how does such characterization construct concepts and classifications in the narrative's construction of meaning? In other words, what is the cultural expression emanating from the literary text by the implied author in the perspective of the interpreter? What sort of reflection in terms of concepts and classifications is occurring when characters are interpreted? The assumption here is that representation is interrelated with discourse and power. Thus, there is a link between the representations emanating from the interpretation of characters in the text and how racial/ethnic, gender, class, or religious representations today are understood. In a similar way, if one takes the American Western Museum as a text, the objects or paintings on display at the American West (e.g., in the 1800s) play a role in how we view the actors in the history of the American West. Museums, like literary texts, produce systems of representation. Understanding how they do so as well as the politics of narration (or exhibition) are important moves in an ideological approach.

A look at both the poetics and politics of representation through characterization calls for a larger study in greater detail. In what follows, rather than looking at every character in John, I will provide a brief look at three groups of characters ("the Jews," women, and the world) to introduce the issues related to their characterization. In the process, I will also touch upon some ideological issues of representation.

"The Jews"

The question surrounding the identity of "the Jews" (*hoi Ioudaioi*) begins with the multiple negative representations and vitriolic statements directed toward "the Jews" throughout the Fourth Gospel. They are presented as violent (e.g., 5:18; 7:1; 19:7), unbelieving (5:37, 45; 19:15), and demonic (8:44). Such representations and statements against "the Jews" lead to the thought that the Gospel writer(s) might indeed have an issue with this particular group. The repetitive use of the designation "the Jews" in opposition to the Johannine Jesus as well as their characterization as unbelievers have contributed and continue to contribute to an anti-Jewish view and problematic treatment of the Jewish community. Thus, a question for readers is, how would they respond to the negative portrayal of "the Jews" in the Gospel? This question has led scholars over the years to find an explanation for John's apparent anti-Jewish perspective toward this group (Myers 2017). Interestingly, it has led Christian scholars in particular to search for an explanation without compromising the sacred status of the Gospel as part of the Christian canon or people's belief in the Gospel. Along these lines, why might John have employed this designation of "the Jews" to describe Jesus's opponents? To get at a response, scholars often turn to translation theory, even if they do not come to the same conclusion.

Translation and Meaning of
hoi Ioudaioi ("the Jews")

Translation theory is one approach scholars employ to identify *hoi Ioudaioi* ("the Jews") in the Gospel. The designation *hoi Ioudaioi* has about seventy occurrences in the Gospel, compared to five or six times in the Synoptic Gospels (Brown 1966: LXXI). The references function to not only name but also describe or define something about the group. In some instances, "the Jews" or *tou Ioudaioi* function as a simple subject or object in a sentence to name or identify a group (e.g., 1:19, *tou Ioudaioi*; 5:10, *hoi Ioudaioi*; 9:22, *tous Ioudaious*). In other occurrences, "the Jews" function as a kind of modifier to describe or define another noun; this is often done with a particular syntactical expression: "x" of the Jews (e.g., "the feast of the Jews," 5:1; "many of the Jews," 11:45; "crowd of the Jews," 12:9). Not all of the occurrences are negative, but the text of John repeatedly uses the designation in its plot as the antagonists who oppose John's Jesus or the viewpoint of the Gospel. As in many plots, the use of repetition functions, then and now, to persuade hearers/readers of a particular image of a group. In the case of "the Jews," that image happens to be a negative one in John: they represent unbelievers.

Translators, for instance, try to minimize this negative image through different translations (e.g., "the leaders," 2:20 [Contemporary English Version]; "they," 2:6 [Living Bible]; "they," 2:20 [New English Bible]). They suggest that the designation "the Jews" is referring to either a collection of people who did not accept Jesus as Messiah or a particular, powerful group among the Jewish people in the first-century Mediterranean world, but it does not mean *all* Jewish people. In other words, the English definite article, "the," does not identify or conceptualize "the Jews" in a definitive and all-inclusive fashion. Besides, as the line of argument goes, Jesus was Jewish, the disciples were Jewish, and there are Jewish supporters of Jesus in the Gospel, so "the Jews" or *hoi Ioudaioi* in John should not be read as a reference to all Jewish persons. Such a line of argumentation does not take into consideration that someone might internalize and reproduce negative representations of one's own group. This might very well be the case of what was happening with "the Jews" in John, whose authorship was presumably Jewish.

Translation is, of course, not without implications. Every time one translates an ancient language or modern language, even if it is one's own, one interprets. Such is also the case when translating *hoi Ioudaioi*. Some scholars have argued that *hoi Ioudaioi*, similar to the word "the world" (*cosmos*) in John, can be translated in multiple ways. One possible translation is "Judeans" rather than "the Jews." The argument for "Judeans" rests on the supposition that the designation *hoi Ioudaioi* is referring to those Jewish folks living in Jerusalem and the region of Judea. It is not a term pointing to *all* Jewish folks in the ancient Mediterranean world. Scholars who lean toward "Judeans" for *hoi Ioudaioi* are emphasizing the designation's geographical meaning, thus linking a people and land—such as Samaritans from Samaria or Galileans from Galilee (e.g., see Jn 11–12). We can see here, therefore, that scholars may interpret *hoi Ioudaioi* as referring to the entire land of ancient Israel as well as to a specific region within (Cohen 1999: 72–8). Some also interpret *hoi Ioudaioi* as an ethnic designation, such as Greeks and Romans. The problem with an ethnic–geographic understanding of *hoi Ioudaioi* is that it does not take into account that the designation's meaning might change over time. Some have argued that during the composition of the Gospel, the term *hoi Ioudaioi* changed to include not just an ethnic–geographical meaning but also a religious one (Cohen 1999: 70; Sheridan 2013: 689). This instability opens the door for other possibilities.

Another common translation of *hoi Ioudaioi* is Jewish authorities. Scholars reach this conclusion by observing those occurrences of *hoi Ioudaioi* (e.g., 5:18; 7:13; 9:22) that appear to convey the meaning of a religious leadership. That is, by analyzing the narrative context where *hoi Ioudaioi* is employed in the Gospel and by making comparisons ("objectively?") to other uses of *hoi Ioudaioi*, a different understanding is suggested. Instead of an ethnic–geographic designation, these scholars draw the conclusion that *hoi Ioudaioi* really means Jewish authorities. For instance, in Jn 5:10, 15, and 18, *hoi Ioudaioi* plays a role as interrogators and judges, the same roles ascribed to the Pharisees or chief priests based on historical/literary material. To support this position, scholars point to the Gospel's compositional history to show that *hoi Ioudaioi* reflects a particular period of the Gospel's literary strata where *hoi Ioudaioi* refers to Jewish authorities. In other words, during the composition of John after 70 CE, when Pharisaic Judaism survived Rome's destruction of Jerusalem and the temple, the term *hoi Ioudaioi* came to refer specifically to the Jewish authorities such as the Pharisees and the chief priests. Therefore, the term *hoi Ioudaioi* does not mean all Jewish people, but rather refers to those with religious/cultural power. To support this position even further, scholars compare the Gospel of John to the Synoptic Gospels. Since the Synoptic Gospels include a variety of groups of Jewish people (e.g., the Sadducees, Herodians, Zealots) without referencing all Jews as a single monolithic collective, these scholars argue that *hoi Ioudaioi* should be understood in similar ways. For them, "the Jews" mean specifically those who oppose Jesus to protect their own power and influence. As such, they are those who fall on the negative end of John's dualistic worldview; they are evil, members of darkness, and even liars (Brown 1966: LXXI–LXXII).

All of this is to say that the translation and meaning of the term *hoi Ioudaioi* is unresolved and complex. The term suggests different meanings, depending on how one understands the Gospel's compositional history and its rhetorical representation. Understandings of the textual and historical *hoi Ioudaioi* have, therefore, remained ambiguous and debatable. However, this ambiguity or inconsistency does not take away the rhetorical force of "the Jews" as represented as the evil "other" in John. As mentioned above, the repetitive force of *hoi Ioudaioi* ("the Jews") throughout the Gospel sears an image of them as unenlightened and violent (e.g., 5:18, 37; 19:7).

The continuity of this caustic representation "naturalizes" (in a sacred text!) their representation as reality for some readers, as history continues to show.

Much of the difficulty behind translation and meaning, which is not always taken into consideration, is the identity of the translator or interpreter. The task of interpretation involves not only allowing the text of John to speak for itself (howsoever possible), but also understanding how the subjectivity of the interpreter brings an ideological or theological perspective to one's reading (such as how one understands *hoi Ioudaioi* in John or John's Gospel as a whole). This ideological or theological perspective of an interpreter is seldom analyzed. For instance, for some scholars, the assumption that the Gospel is the result of a Christological debate between believers and unbelievers or between Christians and Jewish folks (see Chapter 1) frames their reading along a polemical perspective. However, those who subscribe to such a hypothesis hardly ever analyze the assumptions that frame their interpretation. Within Johannine studies, there has been very little critical evaluation of the interpreter's identity or the interpreter's ideological commitments to difference or interreligious dialogue. Such an examination of Johannine scholarship is as important as understanding the sociohistorical and literary worlds of John's text. Besides, representation of any group does not occur in a vacuum. Representation of a group or an individual is partially put together by an interpreter, along with the narrator of the text. Such a representation prescribes ways for talking about groups and individuals as well as how to treat them across space and time.

Because of this complexity and ambiguity, some scholars, including me, decide to translate *hoi Ioudaioi* as "the Jews," enclosed with double quotation marks to indicate the difficulty in translating and interpreting the term (Reinhartz 2001). Ideological commitments against racism, anti-Judaism, and dualistic constructions of reality (where identities are grouped in an either/or framework) also inform my reading of "the Jews." Such a position calls for a critical engagement with the Gospel as well as other sacred texts that connect the divine–human spirit of the past with the divine–human spirit of today for self-understanding in the present. In this way, the negative representation of "the Jews" is not erased from the narrative text, for it was a cultural expression of its time, but this representation needs to be placed alongside other representations in the Gospel (such as that of women) as well as contemporary experiences and interpretations (Reinhartz 2001).

Women in the Gospel

Similar to "the Jews," the representation of women in the Gospel of John is debated and unsettled among scholars. On the one hand, women characters play important roles in various stories in the Gospel and are represented as coequals of men (Schüssler-Fiorenza 1984; Schneiders 1999; Kysar 2007). On the other hand, women characters are interpreted as supporters of the Johannine Jesus (e.g., Jesus as the messianic bridegroom), thus reifying the patriarchal and androcentric structures of society (Fehribach 1998). In addition to interpretations that read women in John as either positive or negative, others have suggested that the portrayal of women in John is ambiguous or in process (Conway 2002; Hylen 2009). Still others have argued that women in John must not be read in isolation; instead, their portrayal must be read alongside that of men (Conway 1999) or in light of Sophia as a female figure, including Sophia's role in the portrayal of Jesus (Scott 1992).

My particular look at the role of women from a literary–ideological perspective in this chapter will focus on a positive characterization of women in John, given how negative characterizations of women continue to dominate popular representations of women. This is not to suggest, of course, that John's Gospel does not contain any negative portrayal of women, or that women in John cannot be read negatively. I choose positive characterizations over negative characterizations to highlight significant elements of their role in the plot development of John.

The Mother of Jesus (2:1-11; 19:25-28)

The mother of Jesus, who is unnamed in this Gospel, appears in two narrative passages (2:1-11 and 19:25-28) within the first Jerusalem/Galilee cycle (1:19–3:36) and the last cycle to Jerusalem (18:1–21:25), respectively. In the first occurrence, the narrative context is a wedding that takes place in Cana in Galilee (2:1) on the third day, that is, two days after Jesus's calling of disciples (1:19-51). Thus, the wedding-at-Cana story is the first public scene in the ministry of Jesus. Furthermore, present at the wedding are the mother of Jesus, Jesus and his disciples, guests (implied), servants, a steward; consequently, it could be argued that the mother of Jesus is accompanying Jesus on his ministry and beyond (2:12).

The issue at the center of this story is that the wine ran out at the wedding. For some reason the mother of Jesus is feeling responsible as host or perhaps a close friend of the host. Recognizing Jesus's identity as the Son of God who possesses the power to do something, she informs Jesus that all the wine has been consumed: "They have no wine" (2:3). Jesus's following response has sparked all sorts of interpretation: "Woman, what concern is that to you and to me? My hour has not yet come" (2:4b-d). One question for scholars is whether the word "woman" (*gunai*), which is in the vocative case in Greek, is a simple or emphatic address. The word appears here without the particle (*ho*, "the"), so it reads like a simple address. If it did have the particle before it (*ho gunai*), it could be translated as "O woman" and understood as conveying an emphatic sense of rebuke. But there are occasions in the New Testament when the particle is not included and the emphatic/rebuke force remains in the context (e.g., Mk 1:24, Mt. 4:10, Lk. 4:34). Jesus's response is closer to a rebuke if one takes the narrative context into consideration. Jesus's expression, "what concern is that to you and to me" (2:4c), conveys a coarse or a harsh reprimand. Jesus's following words, "My hour has not yet come" (2:4d), perhaps suggest that he does not do things because others want him to do them; rather, he only does those things that are God's will and in God's timing. What one emphasizes, grammar or narrative context or both, will influence the interpretation, not to mention if one reads Jesus's mother's response in the following verse ("His mother said to the servants, 'Do whatever he tells you,'" 2:5a) as conveying a sense of offense or a sense of respect. In any case, the servants do exactly what the mother commands and what Jesus instructs them to do: "Fill the jars with water" (2:7b). Afterward, the water miraculously becomes wine (2:9). It leads to a recognition of his identity and confirms the disciples' and others' faith in Jesus (2:11).

It is challenging to know for sure whether Jesus is rebuking his mother or not at this point of the narrative. Most interpretations are approximations based on literary and historical texts ("evidence") with similar grammatical constructions or expressions. The representation of Jesus's mother here is complex and conflicted. She still seems ambivalent about Jesus's full identity, since she tries to override God's will ("My hour has not yet come," 2:4c), but she did jumpstart Jesus's public ministry. Her characterization becomes even more complex when we read this text (2:1-12) in relation to another text where the mother of Jesus appears (20:25). In this later text, she is at the foot of the cross with other women, expressing courage, not to mention full recognition of Jesus while Jesus is dying and when most of the male disciples (except the Beloved Disciple) are away in hiding. In this context, the mother of Jesus is represented positively for sure; the Gospel emphasizes her loyalty, despite any negative representation of her that may have been present in Jn 2. The narrative sequence seems to redefine her characterization as Jesus's mother: from one who does not really understand her son (not like Jesus's Father does) to one who truly understands her son (like the Father does).

Samaritan Woman (4:1-42)

To understand the Samaritan woman, some scholars opt to study her in relationship to Nicodemus in Jn 3 (Conway 1997). The comparative look between these characters highlights their identities. For instance, Nicodemus is a Pharisee (3:1) and the woman is a Samaritan (4:7); Nicodemus comes at night (3:2) and the woman comes during the day (4:6); Nicodemus is a secret disciple (7:50; 19:38) and the woman becomes a spokesperson for her community. Such comparative analysis has lots of merit and contributes to our understanding of the Samaritan woman.

The Samaritan woman, like the mother of Jesus in John, is unnamed. Scholars have likened the story to a type scene of betrothal that is found over and over again in the biblical text (Gen. 24:11; 29:2; Exod. 2:16). The betrothal type scene refers to a story of a man meeting a woman at a well: he does something nice there for the woman, she goes and tells her family, the man is then invited for a meal, an exchange of gifts occurs, and, finally, the two go off and get married. In Jn 4, the betrothal type scene, more or less, is as follows: the Samaritan woman meets Jesus at the well, Jesus gives her a gift ("living water"), she goes and tells her community, and she and the Samaritans recognize and welcome Jesus. But, with all type scenes, one should not overlook matters pertaining to gender and sexuality.

The traditional representation of the Samaritan woman is that she is a sinner because of her sex life or her pattern of relationship (4:16-18). However, the Johannine Jesus never passes judgment upon the woman; he simply confirms her response to his command:

> Jesus said to her, "Go, call your husband, and come back." The woman answered him, "I have no husband." Jesus said to her, "You are right in saying, 'I have no husband'; for you have had five husbands, and the one you have now is not your husband." "What you have said is true!" The woman said to him, "Sir, I see that you are a prophet." (4:16-19)

There is no direct critical opinion against the Samaritan woman with regard to her sexual history; rather it appears—it can be argued—that what Jesus is really doing here is showing his omniscience as he did with Nathanael (cf. 1:48-49). In other words, Jesus discloses the private life of the Samaritan woman in order to demonstrate who he is. His aim is to bring her to recognition of his true identity. The Samaritan, therefore, is not the sexual sinner as she is often claimed to be, she is quite sharp and powerful in her engagement with Jesus. From the beginning of the story, the Samaritan woman questions the cultural taboo of a Jewish man requesting a drink from a Samaritan woman (4:9); it is deemed improper because of her "racialized" identity and her being alone in public as a "sexualized" female. She also questions Jesus's identity as the source of living water (4:11), and she even pushes him theologically by questioning his authority in relationship to Jacob (4:12). Thus, the representation of the Samaritan woman—as I see it—is not one who serves as a foil in the text to reveal Jesus's identity, but rather a representation that works against popular racialized and gendered representation (Samaritan woman cannot speak and is not equal to Jewish men). By questioning Jesus, the Samaritan woman makes explicit what is often hidden: the racialized and sexualized power differentials between Jesus and the Samaritan woman.

Taking a different turn, the Samaritan woman, as some scholars with a postcolonial perspective have convincingly suggested to readers, is one who is used by the Johannine Jesus in colonial ways (Dube 1996; Kim 2004). The Samaritan woman does come to recognize Jesus (4:19-26) and, in so doing, the Samaritan woman concedes her traditional place of worship (4:20), leaves her everyday life (4:28), and goes to her community to witness to Jesus as the Messiah (4:39-42). Thus, because of the woman's testimony of Jesus, the Samaritans acknowledge Jesus as the "Savior of the world"—a title often used in reference to the Roman emperor. In other words, the Samaritan woman plays the role of the "converted one" who brings faith to her community. Following this line of thinking, the representation of the Samaritan woman is one who plays the role of the colonized—her land and religion are usurped, her way of life is considered inferior, and her community is assimilated or colonized by the Johannine Savior (4:19-42). In this light, Jesus's offering of living water (or eternal life) is simply colonial poison for it kills one off from one's identity and land.

Thus, the story of the Samaritan woman raises many questions and leads to various interpretations, depending on the lens employed by the interpreter. What these interpretations show is the ambiguities of racial/ ethnic and gender representation. It is important to acknowledge and analyze these representations critically to avoid reifying "racialized" and "sexualized" gender representations as "natural."

The Adulterous Woman (or the Sexualized Woman)

A text that is often bypassed by scholars in the analysis of Johannine women is the story traditionally labeled "The Adulterous Woman" (7:53–8:11). The reason why the story is not included in many modern English and Spanish versions of John or why the story is often circumvented altogether within the Johannine tradition has to do with its absence from the earliest manuscripts (with the exception of Codex Bezae [D] from the fifth century) of the Gospel of John; nor is it referred to by the earlier church leaders. There are other reasons for dismissing 7:53–8:11 in scholarly studies of John: its vocabulary and style of writing are more like Luke's Gospel than John's; the motif of recognition is not furthered in this story, for example. Considering its textual history, the question of whether to include this story in the final form of John or even in a section about the women of John remains problematic. While this episode's textual history remains problematic, it needs to be engaged and not avoided. As in all narrativizations of history (see Chapter 1), silences in history and narrative are often telling.

The story of the adulterous woman has often been reduced to the woman's adultery but the man in this adulterous relationship is not even mentioned (Guardiola-Sáenz 2002). Such traditional interpretations have "sexualized" the woman, that is, they have assumed that the woman, because she is a woman, is "naturally" the seducer and hence responsible for the adultery. Other interpretations of the story focus on the theme of forgiveness and reconciliation, but the "adulterous" woman is portrayed as the foil that leads to this theme. However, the Johannine Jesus, in his attempt to keep the accusers of the "adulterous" woman from stoning her to death, shifts the focus away from her and onto the accusers who, presumably in ways similar to the sinful woman, cannot claim to be without sin (8:7-9). Jesus, now alone with her, does not condemn her, but commands her not to sin anymore. Thus, Jesus shows mercy upon her; he, as many commentators have suggested, condemns her sin but not her person. Such an interpretation still reads the "adulterous" woman as the problem, rather than analyzing those laws or socioreligious practices and attitudes that the dominant group (men in patriarchy) takes for granted and employs to accuse the woman but excuse the man in this "adulterous" relationship. Through this interpretive focus on forgiveness and reconciliation, the woman is presented negatively as a sinful and shameless temptress; she remains trapped within male gaze and fantasy. In fact, her voice is nearly absent in the text. Her only words are, when she says in response to Jesus's question of whether anyone has condemned her, "No one, sir" (8:11). She is stereotypically represented as the "female other" within a patriarchal culture; her story and interpretations of it say more about the patriarchal influence of the past and of the present.

Mary and Martha of Bethany (11:1-46; 12:1-8)

Employing a literary–ideological perspective, the representations of Mary and Martha have led scholars to see them as faithful disciples. Yet, despite Martha's confession and Mary's actions, their faithfulness in Jesus is not lacking in ambiguity (Hylen 2009: 77–91). They do not understand everything Jesus says and, in the case with Mary, she gives no explicit confession of Jesus's identity similar to the one articulated by Martha (11:27). Their representations have also led to interpretations that see them as embodying the patriarchal expectations of women at the time: they express their love of Jesus, they serve Jesus, and they assume the emotional grief of their community (Fehribach 1998: 83–113).

One can argue, however, that representations of both Mary and Martha expand the range of gender representations; they challenge any reductionist representation of female as merely accommodating and emotional.

Martha is the first woman to fully recognize Jesus as the Christ (11:27); her confession is similar to those given by John the Baptist (1:34), Andrew (1:41), Nathanael (1:49), and Peter (6:69). The Samaritan woman also somewhat confesses, but not with the same boldness as Martha (cf. 4:29). For sure, Martha is represented here as a self-confident leader like the other disciples. She is the initiator, if you will, between the two sisters. She goes to Jesus while Mary remains at home (11:20). Like her sister Mary, Martha draws on her friendship with Jesus as well as Jesus's friendship with Lazarus to move Jesus to raise Lazarus from the dead. Furthermore, when Mary meets Jesus, she shows belief by falling on her feet and saying the same words to Jesus as Martha did: "Lord, if you had been here, my brother would not have died" (11:32; cf. 11:21).

When Mary comes, a group of mourners (interestingly called "the Jews") also go with her (11:31). Jesus is "greatly disturbed in spirit and deeply moved" (11:33) when he sees them. He is so moved that he begins to weep (11:35). Both Mary and Martha in this narrative are represented positively as self-confident leaders as well as being accommodating and emotional. Even though the last sign of John's Gospel—the raising of Lazarus from the dead—is also done by Jesus, these two women, similar to the mother of Jesus with the first sign, are the ones who make the first move to initiate the miracle.

In the second narrative that features Mary and Martha (12:1-8), Mary shows her faith in Jesus through her actions instead of through her words, as she did in the first episode. In Bethany, at the home of Lazarus, who has now been raised, Mary and Martha host a dinner for Jesus. At the dinner, Mary brings costly perfume and anoints Jesus's feet and wipes them with her hair; unknowingly, she prepares for Jesus's death and burial. Such action shows her affection and gratitude toward Jesus. At the same time, Judas, who will betray Jesus, objects to Mary's lavishness and falsely insinuates that the money could have been given to the poor (12:6). In this episode, Martha characteristically serves and Mary anoints Jesus's feet—not his whole body (cf. Mt. 26:12 and Mk 14:8)—with her hair (not with a towel, cf. 13:4) as an act of service (Hylen 2009: 87). Both acts of service show loyalty and thus are portrayed positively from John's point of view.

These two narratives—along with others in the Gospel—challenge patriarchal understandings of discipleship and leadership. The women, as others have pointed out, are leaders within the emerging Johannine community. Mary and Martha's gender representations are expanded to include multiple possibilities in both the public and private spheres. In short, both Mary and Martha emerge as women leaders who recognize Jesus, but whether their recognition is full or partial is open to discussion. How they are interpreted will undoubtedly have an effect on women's roles in both the ecclesial tradition and our society at large.

Mary Magdalene (20:1-18)

Mary Magdalene is also often viewed positively as a faithful disciple, for she is the first one in the story of John to bring the news of the empty tomb to Peter and the Beloved Disciple (20:2). She truly represents what it means to be a disciple (Brown 1966: 189–90). She is not only a supporter of Jesus at the foot of the cross alongside the mother of Jesus and the Beloved Disciple (19:25-30); she also exemplifies fidelity, love, openness, and witness (Kysar 2007: 152).

Mary Magdalene discovers an empty tomb and concludes that the body of Jesus has been taken away (20:2). After being informed by Mary Magdalene, Peter and the Beloved Disciple run to the empty tomb and see Jesus's head cloth lying separately from the clothes but very carefully rolled up by itself. The disciples conclude from this, according to the narrator, that Jesus has not been taken away but that he has resurrected (20:9). In contrast to the disciples who view the empty tomb in terms of resurrection, Mary Magdalene sees it in terms of Jesus's body being stolen; this shows that her understanding of Jesus, at this point of the story, has not reached a point of full recognition. As the story develops, however, Mary Magdalene does refer to Jesus as "Lord" and assumes that he is the Son of God (20:18). She does eventually reach full recognition.

Mary Magdalene is also the first person in the story to whom the resurrected Jesus reveals himself (20:11-18). While the disciples return to their homes, Mary Magdalene remains at the tomb in tears and, as she weeps, she looks into the tomb and discovers two angels who ask her why she is crying. After a brief reply to the angels' question, Mary turns away from the tomb and sees Jesus standing there, but she does not recognize him, thinking that he is a gardener (20:15). She continues in this state of nonrecognition with further questions of Jesus's whereabouts; it is not until Jesus addresses her as Mary that she comes to full recognition. Like the good shepherd who calls on one's sheep by name, Jesus calls Mary by name and she responds to him as "*Rabboni*" or "Teacher." Mary Magdalene tries to hold on to Jesus but Jesus refuses, for he has not ascended to God (20:17). Consequently, Mary Magdalene departs and tells the good news to the disciples, thus preparing the disciples for Jesus's appearance to them (20:24-29).

In terms of characterization, Mary Magdalene's announcement to the disciples after the discovery of the empty tomb (20:2) and after she recognizes Jesus (20:18) strongly suggests that she is not only faithful but also a leader who carries news about Jesus to the believing community. Like many of the other disciples (21:4), with the exception of the Beloved Disciple, she also shows ambivalence regarding the identity of the resurrected Jesus until Jesus calls her by name. Some argue that Mary Magdalene represents a frantic female who has lost her lover, especially in the beginning of the narrative (20:1-10) and that she assumes a prophetic role only after she recognizes the resurrected Jesus (Fehribach 1998: 143–67). In contrast, Mary Magdalene as an eyewitness of Jesus's resurrection (and of his crucifixion in 19:4) leads some to suggest that perhaps she is really the Beloved Disciple or even the author of John (Schneiders 1999: 211–32).

As expected, the interpretations of Mary Magdalene, as with those of the other women in John, vary, depending on who is doing the interpretation and what literary aspects on which interpreters wish to focus in the narrative. What is interesting is that these interpretations, including my own, strongly lean toward a more positive portrayal of the women characters in John, even if these female roles seem to be situated within ancient patriarchal norms. For example, the Samaritan woman acts against the cultural norms (Samaritan women and Jewish men are not supposed to speak to each other) and thus makes explicit the racialized and sexualized assumptions that are often hidden and hence rarely discussed.

The World

A third group of characters often overlooked in reading John is the "world" (*kosmos*). The word "world" appears in John seventy-eight times with several connotations. One such connotation of the "world" appears to refer to all human beings and the whole creation. In the Gospel's prologue, specifically 1:9-10, the "world" signifies a place where the Logos moves (from the world above and to the world below, 1:9c, 10a). As the physical cosmos, the "world" is the result and the proof of the Word's creative capacity (1:10b). In the sense of the "world" as human beings, the world has the choice to recognize the Logos or not (1:10c). Thus, the meaning of the "world" is constantly in flux in John. To receive a better sense of its meanings, a look at various places in the story where the "world" is seen positively, negatively, or ambiguously will be beneficial.

When John uses the "world" in an affirming way, the "world" seems to refer either to creation itself (whole creation) or the world of humans (world below). For instance, in 1:9, the "world" refers to the whole creation; one can also find this same sense of meaning in 17:5, 24 and 21:25. In 17:5c, in Jesus's Farewell Prayer in John, Jesus prays that God would return him to the glory of God's presence; this is the same glory that Jesus as Logos shared with God before the "world" came into existence. In 17:24e, this sense of "the world" as the whole creation appears again with a spatial connotation that suggests a place or created world ("before the foundation of the world"). And finally, in 21:25c, the last verse of John, the "world" refers to all of creation ("I suppose that the world itself could not contain the books that would be written"). In all these examples (1:9; 17:5, 24; 21:25), the "world" is used in an affirming fashion; it is seen as the location where God works, thus providing the "world" with an intrinsic worth or value.

The value of the "world" is generally affirmed when it refers to humans (e.g., 1:10; 3:16; 7:4; 8:12), but this "world" of humans either receives or rejects Jesus. In that well-known and oft-cited verse from John's Gospel—"For God so loved the world that God gave God's only Son" (3:16)—God is clearly shown to value the "world" of humans, but this "world" is also clearly in need of God's love. John 1:10c points out that this "world" of humans has failed to recognize Jesus ("yet the world knew him not"). In 7:4a, the "world" also refers to humans who oppose Jesus ("The world cannot hate you, but it hates me"). But in 8:12b, the Johannine Jesus says he is the light of the "world," and those who follow him will have life. In all these instances, the "world" refers to humans, but these humans need to recognize Jesus as the Light/Son of God. In a subtle way, one could argue that this particular sense of the "world" as humans is seen as needing "salvation." The world is one that may not recognize Jesus, which explains its hostility toward Jesus, but this "world" was made through Jesus/Logos with the ability to know Jesus. The "world" is one that is made up of different peoples, and these peoples will either receive "salvation" (e.g., 3:17; 7:7; 12:31; 16:20, 33) or be condemned. This does not mean that the "world" is necessarily something negative; rather, the "world," as suggested above, is the object of God's love (Kysar 2007: 61).

Why John uses the "world" in multiple ways (i.e., creation, humanity, an ethical universe capable of making decisions) is difficult to say for sure, but like "the Jews" and the women in John, the "world" in John is a character that, depending on interpreters and interpretations, carries various implications. Readers or interpreters are caught up in a play of power, unconsciously or consciously, as they struggle over the meaning of character representation in John, since their reading or interpretation often contributes to our culturally constructed identities and a sense of who we are. In other words, representation of characters occupies a central place in our reading of John. With the potential of organizing and regulating theological and social practices, our readings of John may influence society's conduct and, consequently, may have real and practical social effects on different groups of people.

References

Bennema, C. (2013), "A Comprehensive Approach to Understanding Character in the Gospel of John," in C. W. Skinner (ed.), *Characters*

and *Characterization in the Gospel of John*, LNTS 461, 36–58,
New York: T&T Clark.

Brown, R. E. (1966), *The Gospel According to John*, Anchor Bible 29,
New York: Doubleday.

Cohen, S. J. D. (1999), *The Beginnings of Jewishness: Boundaries, Varieties,
Uncertainties*, Berkeley: University of California Press.

Conway, C. M. (1999), *Men and Women in the Fourth Gospel: Gender and
Johannine Characterization*, SBL Dissertation Series 167, Atlanta: Society of
Biblical Literature.

Conway, C. M. (2002), "Speaking through Ambiguity: Minor Characters in the
Fourth Gospel," *Biblical Interpretation* 10: 324–41.

Dube, M. W. (1996), "Reading for Decolonization (John 4:1-42)," *Semeia*
75: 37–59.

Fehribach, A. (1998), *The Women in the Life of the Bridegroom: A Feminist
Historical-Literary Analysis of the Female Characters in the Fourth Gospel*,
Collegeville: Liturgical Press.

Guardiola-Sáenz, L. A. (2002), "Border-crossing and Its Redemptive Power
in John 7.53–8.11: A Cultural Reading of Jesus and the *Accused*," in M.
W. Dube and J. L. Staley (eds.), *John and Postcolonialism: Travel, Space
and Power*, The Bible and Postcolonialism, 7, 129–52, Sheffield: Sheffield
Academic Press.

Hylen, S. E. (2009), *Imperfect Believers: Ambiguous Characters in the Gospel of
John*, Louisville, KY: Westminster John Knox Press.

Kim, J. K. (2004), *Woman and Nation: An Intercontextual Reading of the Gospel
of John from a Postcolonial Feminist Perspective*, Leiden: Brill.

Kysar, R. (2007), *John, The Maverick Gospel*, 3rd ed., Louisville,
KY: Westminster John Knox Press.

Myers, A. D. (2012), *Characterizing Jesus: A Rhetorical Analysis on the
Fourth Gospel's Use of Scripture in Its Presentation of Jesus*, LNTS 458,
New York: T&T Clark.

Myers, A. D. (2017), "Just Opponents? Ambiguity, Empathy, and the Jews
in the Gospel of John," in S. Brown and C. W. Skinner (eds.), *Johannine
Ethics: The Moral World of the Gospel and Epistles of John*, 159–76,
Minneapolis, MN: Fortress Press.

Reinhartz, A. (2001), *Befriending the Beloved Disciple*, New York: Continuum.

Schneiders, S. M. (1999), *Written That You May Believe: Encountering Jesus in
the Fourth Gospel*, New York: Crossroad.

Schüssler-Fiorenza, E. (1984), *In Memory of Her: A Feminist-Theological
Reconstruction of Christian Origins*, New York: Crossroad.

Scott, M. (1992), *Sophia and the Johannine Jesus*, Journal for the Study of the
Old Testament, Supplement Series 212, Sheffield: Sheffield Academic Press.

Sheridan, R. (2013), "Issues in the Translations of οἱ Ἰουδαῖοι in the Fourth
Gospel," *Journal of Biblical Literature* 132, no. 3: 671–95.

Further Reading

Bennema, C. (2014), *Encountering Jesus: Character Studies in the Gospel of John*, 2nd ed., Minneapolis, MN: Fortress Press.

Brown, R. E. (1979), *The Community of the Beloved Disciple*, New York: Paulist Press.

Goss, R. E. (2006), "John," in D. Guest, R. E. Goss, and M. West (eds.), *The Queer Bible Commentary*, 548–65, London: SCM.

Okure, T. (1988), *The Johannine Approach to Mission: A Contextual Study of John 4:1-42*, Wissenschafliche Untersuchungen zum Neuen Tetament 2/31, Tübingen: Mohr Siebeck.

Seim, T. K. (1987), "Roles of Women in the Gospel of John," in L. Hartman and B. Olsson (eds.), *John and the Synoptics*, 56–73, Uppsala: Almqvist & Wiksell.

Skinner, C. W. (ed.) (2014), *Characters and Characterization in the Gospel of John*, LNTS 416, London: Bloomsbury T&T Clark.

4

John 1:1-18: A World Split Apart

Chapter Outline

Introduction 74
At Home—The World Above: 1:1-2 74
The Word's Crossing: 1:3-17 76
Returning Home—The World Above: 1:18 82
Conclusion 83
References 84
Further Reading 84

As seen in the last two chapters, understanding the various literary aspects of John entails understanding aspects of the story of John (the plot) as well as elements of its discourse (e.g., characterization). Another path to take is by way of a close reading of a particular text within the Gospel from a literary–ideological perspective. A close reading of the Gospel's narrative of beginnings or prologue (1:1-18) in this chapter provides an illustration, although brief, of getting at John's literary construction through its narrative "episodes." The following reading focuses on the text itself, suspending any direct engagement with other literary–ideological readings or with any sociohistorical questions. Nonetheless, no reading is done in a vacuum. Thus, this reading is the result of coverage in the classroom as well as previous readings on 1:1-18 over the years (e.g., Brown 1966; Moloney 1993; Culpepper 1998; Segovia 2002). What is more, with a focus on selective words, syntax, and order of 1:1-18 (i.e., a close reading approach), the reading also aims to explore the cultural expression that emanates from such close reading. By calling for a particular way of life as well as identity, this cultural expression may carry resultant effects on perceived reality, values, and understandings of who belongs and who does not belong in a community or society.

Introduction

The prologue of John can be delimited in many ways, but in this reading of the prologue, as in the reading of the plot of the Gospel, the journey motif will shape the three narrative sections, leading to a focus on the world above (1:1-2); the world below (1:3-17); and back to the world above (1:18). The entire narrative division, 1:1-18, which is also a narrative unit itself, is part of a divisional outline of the Gospel as a whole: 1:1-18; 1:19–17:26; and 18:1–21:25 (Segovia 1991). Informing the divisional outline of the Gospel here is a human migration motif: the movement of leaving a sending place, crossing borders and waters, and establishing a permanent or a temporary commitment to a receiving place. This pattern is reflected in Jesus's movement in John. For this reading, it is difficult to escape the reality of mass migrations across the globe—and all of the related issues, such as violence—in reading John (Jones 2017). Thus, I am calling these divisions a narrative of unsettlement (1:1-18), a narrative of travel/crossing (1:19–17:26), and a narrative of resettlement (18:1–21:25). And as seen in Chapter 1, what stirs this movement is the motif of recognition of the Word, with the resultant effects of featuring a particular way of life and identity.

At Home—The World Above: 1:1-2

The section opens with three identity factors about the Word (*logos*). After introducing the Word as the subject of the division/unit, the first verse presents its temporal setting (1:1a), its physical relationship with God (1:1b), and its spiritual or theological relationship with God (1:1c)—all in the world above: "In the beginning was the Word, and the Word was with God, and the Word was God." In the first independent clause (1:1a), the temporal setting of the prologue is established. The Word has existed since the beginning of time: "In the beginning." For sure, as many commentators have suggested, the word "beginning" (*archē*) takes readers/hearers back to Gen. 1:1, the time before creation. It is signaling that the subject of the clause, "the Word" (*ho logos*), has existed before the world was created, and the imperfect verb "was" (*ēn*) suggests that the Word did not just come into being at one particular occasion but that it continues to exists. In addition to the Word existing before the created world and time, the Word is also in a close association with God: "and the Word was with God" (1:1b). Again, the prologue uses an imperfect verb, "was" (*ēn*), to link the subject and the verb, and this time the verb is pointing to the close proximity between the Word and God. The Word is distinct from God—signaled by the definite article, "the" (*ton*)—but the Word is also with (*pros*) God in the world above. Finally, besides pointing to the Word's spatial location, the Word is divine: "and the Word was God" (1:1c). The verb links the subject, the Word, with God, and this time the verb also expresses the nature of their relationship. In other words, the Word shares the nature of God; the Word is fully God. Thus, with one sentence, the prologue opens up an elaborate description of the identity of the Word. The Word's temporal, physical, and theological identity is delineated in such a way that not only defines the Word's spatial identity (the world above or the Word's place of birth) but also introduces the subject that will solicit acceptance and rejection from the world.

To underscore the prologue's work to delineate the Word's identity and origin, the section reiterates the Word's temporal, physical, and divine relationship with God: "He was in the beginning with God" (1:2). Once again, we learn that the Word exists before time and creation, the Word is above with God, and the Word is close to God. All of these elements are descriptive identity markers that will serve to explain the Word's engagement with believers and unbelievers later in the story. However, the first two verses do not stop with simply presenting the Word's background. They also convey a cultural expression of the world in relation to the Word.

First, the Word is superior over others: it is before everything; second, the Word is above all since the Word is with God; and third, the Word is powerful since the Word is God. In all three expressions, several representations, ideologically speaking, of reality are presented: priority (the Word, as mentioned, existed before all things and nothing existed before the Word), hierarchy (the Word is above all), and authority (the Word is God over other gods). What is more, this Word as God is male through the use of the demonstrative pronoun "he" (*houtos*)—a third-person masculine pronoun—and thus a patriarchal world is also envisioned. Thus, in speaking about the Word's identity, a conceptual world of priority, hierarchy, authority, and patriarchy is envisioned by the text, even though these cultural "ideals" are not explicitly named. The existence of the Johannine Word assumes a *particular* conceptual world.

The Word's Crossing: 1:3-17

While the first section has taken the reader back to Gen. 1, the section continues to expand this intertextual move. It begins with a focus on the Word's identity as Creator: "All things came into being through him, and without him not one thing came into being" (1:3a-b). By doing so, the point of view of the text shifts from the world above toward the created world below.

In the first clause (1:3a), the prologue effectively expresses that the Word is the source of all of creation—"all things" (*panta*)—and that all of this creation came or was created through him (*di' autou egeneto*) as the instrument of creation: "and without him not one thing came into being." This second clause (1:3b) reiterates the point by articulating the consequences of the Word's inaction rather than its action. In other words, the second clause maintains that the Word is the means of creation but it does so by emphasizing (through negation) that nothing is created without the Word as the creative agent. For sure, the Word is the creator of all things; as Creator, the Word is above all and superior over all.

Staying with this theme of identifying the Word as Creator, the prologue expands the Word's creative distinctiveness. The prologue colors the Word with other attributes: "What has come into being in him was life, and the life was the light of all people" (1:3c-4). Overlooking the Greek and English punctuation issues in this sentence that are dealt with in most commentaries, let me state that this agent of creation is now credited for giving life (*zōē*) to all things. As subject nominative of the first clause, life (the Word) is what produces life. In addition, expressed in the second clause, this life (Word) was (*ēn*) the light (*phōs*) of "men" (*anthrōpōn*). (The use of "man" or "men" in this chapter is intentional to highlight John's patriarchal vision.) The imperfect (i.e., continuous) force of "was," again, extends the past into the present, thus the life is the light of humanity now. The vividness of this sentence speaks to the text's interest in presenting the Word in many different ways to capture the completeness of the Word. Using terms like "life" and "light," which appear throughout the Gospel, the text signifies other ideas such as eternity (life) and intellect (light). What remains is the narrator's subtle—or maybe not so subtle—representation of the Word's universal attribute. This is a Word, as life and light, extended to all "men" (*tōn anthrōpōn*); but the text also assumes and promotes a patriarchal world that privileges opportunity for some by restricting opportunity for others.

As life and light, the Word encounters resistance, darkness (*skotia*): "The light shines in the darkness, and the darkness did not overcome it" (1:5). The subject of the one-verse plot is "the light" (*to phōs*) and this "light"—as in Gen. 1—"shines" (*phainei*) now—as expressed with the present tense—and continuously "in the darkness" (*en tē skotia*), which is a completely different sphere than "light." If light is signaling a positive dimension (e.g., knowledge, strength, belief), then darkness is suggesting a negative dimension (e.g., ignorance, weakness, unbelief). The light, therefore, pierces through the darkness, pushing it away. And the result of such action is victory because darkness was unable to "overcome" (*katelaben*, 1:5b) the light. With the second clause, the subject is now "the darkness" (*hē skotia*) and what is expressed is that "the darkness" cannot overcome (or understand, conquer, master) the light, thus suggesting opposition or conflict between "the light" and "the darkness" or between belief and unbelief. This binary tension between light and darkness will be played out in the rest of the section but, more importantly, it will play out throughout the plot of the Gospel with the motif of recognition and nonrecognition. In addition, a hierarchy is reinforced: light is above darkness. Since shifting to the world below, the Gospel begins to unfold its plot: a world filled with darkness that the Word, as light, must overcome to enable those with belief to receive the life that he brings. For those who are in the world below, acceptance and rejection to receive this life (eternity) will be the options from which they may choose.

After concentrating on the Word in relation to creation and humanity, the Word continues his crossing into the world below, with the text now focusing on the Word's human sponsor or advocate. It starts with an introduction to John the Baptist: "There was a man sent from God, whose name was John" (1:6). The statement does several things. First, it introduces another character, a man, besides the Word; secondly, the man has been sent (*apestalmenos*) from God; and thirdly, the man's name is John. This introduction to John, who all of a sudden appears in the text, is on a divine mission—a mission to introduce the Word from above to the world below.

John's mission is to identify the Word: "He came as witness to testify to the light, so that all might believe through him" (1:7). Besides the obvious that the Greek demonstrative pronoun, "he" (*houtos*), is referring to John, the purpose of John is straightforward: he is to give personal testimony or witness—a dominant theme in the Gospel—to the light (the Word). In other words, it is John that paves the way for others to know who the Word is in this Gospel (cf. 1:19-28), and the reason behind this mission is "so that all might believe" in the light (the Word). What the narrator does, therefore, is revealing who the Word is (not to mention John's mission and purpose), as well as disclosing that faith (or belief) in the Word is the issue at hand. John is the witness to the light (or Word), and the response to the Word is one of belief or unbelief ("might believe," *pisteusōsin*).

The narrator is very clear that this man called John is different from the light (or Word). His mission is to give his testimony on behalf of the Word. Thus, the prologue clarifies this point in the following verse, saying: "He himself was not the light, but he came to testify to the light" (1:8). What this text does is to present John as less than the light, but John is still important since his role is to bear witness to the light. The negative particle, "not" (*ouk*), begins the verse in the Greek text, thus stressing this subordinate position held by John in relation to the light. Yet, the verse repeats his purpose: "to testify to the light" (1:8b). Even though both John and the Word were sent from God, the prologue is clear that a hierarchy is present between the two. It is the Word that is the center of the story—not John—and the Word will call on people for a response to either accept or reject the Word. John has a different purpose; his mission is to be a witness to the light (Word).

Since John is not the light, who is the light? The narrator continues to unfold the story of the Word's migration by stressing the subordinate position of John. It does so by identifying the light as "true": "The true light, which enlightens everyone, was coming to the world" (1:9). What the narrator does is identifying the light not as John, but as the true (*alēthinon*) light. The adjective "true" is attributing a quality to the light. The light, thus, is not an inauthentic light and not John, it is the "true light" or the genuine one. This "true light" has a function and that role is to give light to every "man" (*anthrōpon*); this is in keeping with the light's universal but patriarchal vision (cf. 1:4). But just as important as the point about the light's role, the narrator also wants to make it clear that this light "was coming to the world" (1:9c). This is the first explicit indication in the text that the light as the Word is traveling into this world. The use of the present middle participle, "was coming" (*erchomenon*), strongly emphasizes the light's continual journey of descent to the world below. Thus, John is not the light; the light is the Word. And it is the Word who is the true light that enlightens all. What will be revealed in the plot is that some will come to this light (recognition) and some will flee from this light (nonrecognition). The text continues to build a twofold or dualistic worldview.

At this point, the text returns its focus to the light as Word. In so doing, the narrator wishes to explain why the Word is not accepted and, at the same time, the benefits to those who will accept the Word. For the second time, the first time occurring in verse 9, the word "world" is used and it is used to mark the Word's location: "He was in the world, and the world came into being through him, yet the world did not know him" (1:10). The imperfect verb "was" (*ēn*) again is signaling that "he" (the Word)—the person is implied through the verb in the Greek text—continues to exist in the world (1:10a). What is more, as the text reminds its readers, the Word is the agent of all creation: "and the world came into being through him" (1:10b; cf. 1:3). Yet, despite being in the world and despite being the creator of all things, the world fails to accept the Word: "the world did not know him" (1:10c). The world appears to have a choice of either accepting or rejecting the Word. The use of negative particle "not" (*ouk*) and the aorist verb "to know" (*egnō*) emphasizes that the world's nonrecognition of the Word is a reality. Such nonrecognition leads to puncturing any possible meaningful relationship between the Word and the world, unless one accepts the Word.

In the following verse, the encounter of the Word and the world is discussed: "He came to what was his own, and his own people did not accept him" (1:11). In the first clause, the Word travels to "his own" (*ta idia*). Modern commentators have wrestled on how to translate this adjective "his own." Should it be translated as "his own things" (which is a more literal translation) or should it be translated more along the lines of "his own home" (thus signifying a place or a community of people such as the ancient people of Israel)? The latter is what the NRSV as well as other translations suggest, and these translations often make this meaning more obvious by rendering the phrase, "to his own," in the second clause. The Word journeys to his own community and the result is negative; they do not "accept" (*parelabon*) him. In other words, his own community does not welcome or receive him and the verb "accept" functioning as a constative aorist that implies a completed act or bare fact confirms this result. In short, the prologue is foreshadowing the conflict that will occur in the Gospel story proper and reifying the dualistic worlds that will be in conflict with each other in the story: a world of recognition (acceptance) against a world of nonrecognition (rejection).

There are benefits, however, for those who do accept the Word. The narrator mentions that those who receive the Word will be rewarded with a privileged identity or status: "But to all who received him, who believed in his name, he gave power to become children of God" (1:12). The coordinating conjunction "but" (*de*) functioning in a contrastive capacity is stressing that what is to follow is significant. The prologue wants to make it clear regarding those or "all" (*hosoi*) who accept the Word—which means "those who believed" (*tois pisteuousin*) and continue to believe as expressed through the present participle—that the Word "gave them power" (*edōken autois exousian*) to become God's children. Therefore, the text privileges believers with the right to join an exclusive community because of their belief in the Word. Such power to join a community separates them from those communities without such a power. The community that the text speaks about is that of the "children of God" (*tekna theou*). By joining this community, believers share in a special relationship with God and thus occupy a place of belonging in the world above—as opposed to unbelievers who reside in the world below. Such a privilege functions to differentiate people.

To become "children of God" suggests a different notion of family than the conventional biological understanding of family. The "children of God" are those "who were born, not of blood or of the will of the flesh or of the will of man, but of God" (1:13). The prologue is proposing that to be a child of God does not mean being born (*genesthai*) through ancestral descent ("not of blood"); it also has nothing to do with corporeal ("the will of the flesh") or manly desire ("the will of man"). To be a child of God means one is born of God and not by humans. Those who are God's children are born of God. The text, therefore, is calling for a new type of family or community: one that is born of God above over one that is born of blood, flesh, or will below. Again, a bifurcated system of family or community is reinforced.

How this "spiritual" or cosmic birth will happen is through the Word taking on flesh: "And the Word became flesh and lived among us, and we have seen his glory, the glory as of a father's only son, full of grace and truth" (1:14). This notable text in the prologue—especially for the believing community—is the story of the Word's descent or crossing over from the world above to the world below. The Word, creator of all things who gives life and shines light upon all, becomes human flesh. In other words, the Word, the all-powerful one, does not remain in the world above; it journeys below and takes on human life. The verb "became" (*egeneto*) links the subject (Word) with the object (flesh), confirming the Word's action. The Word's identity does not change, the Word still is God; nor does his mission of shining light upon all change. What changes is the Word's appearance and location: he takes on flesh and lives in the world below (1:14a). The decision to live or to dwell (*eskēnōsen*) among humanity suggests that his presence is now among a community of believers and unbelievers. The Word's taking on flesh is his conscious gesture of affection, opening the way for believers to share in his divine presence.

The Word's sojourning to the world below (1:14a) is confirmed through testimony: "and we have seen his glory, the glory as of a father's only son" (1:14b). The narrator, along with others ("we have seen," *etheasametha*), is joining in to witness on behalf of the presence, ministry, and glory of the Word as and in flesh. This glory or divine presence of the Word as flesh is witnessed in the Father's only (*monogenous*) begotten Son. In other words, this Word becoming flesh is God's Son, the only one-of-a-kind son who is an expression of God's glory. He alone is the Son of God, and all others who believe are children of God (cf. 1:13). To confirm this uniqueness, this Son is said to be "full of grace and truth" (1:14c). The modifiers "grace" and "truth," qualified through an additional descriptor ("full," *plērēs*), are important additions to highlight and affirm the Son's actions (grace) and words (truth).

After the narrator's testimony about the Word becoming a man, the text shifts its focus and returns to John the Baptist, who testifies, once again, on behalf of the incarnate Word: "(John testified to him and cried out, 'This was he of whom I said, "He who comes after me ranks ahead of me because he was before me"')" (1:15; English translations typically see this text as an interruption, signaled by enclosing it in parentheses). Nonetheless, this text surely confirms to John's important character role as a witness to the Word or, in this case, the Son of God (1:6-8). What John does is expressive, "he cried out" (*kekragen*) his testimony. John, making his role more explicit, further acknowledges that he is not the one sent by God; nor does he exist before the Son. The Son, who has existed before time, "ranks ahead" (*emprosthen*) of John. Surely, the prologue is clear that there is a separation of identities and roles between the Son and John. The Son is distinct from John, and John, given the only direct discourse in the prologue, confirms the Son's special status.

After this testimony by John, the narrator returns the focus on the Son directly and describes the Son in such a way that highlights his significance: "From his fullness we have all received, grace upon grace" (1:16). The text aims to show that the Son is the source of the infinite "fullness" (*plērōmatos*) that "we" (*hēmeis*), believers, have all experienced or received (*pantes elabomen*). How much fullness? The prologue, through a successive use of "grace"—"grace upon grace" (*charin anti charitos*)—strongly suggests the unbroken series of "grace," so the fullness is boundless. In short, believers are serving as witnesses, as John does, to the Son through their reception of his endless grace. Believers share in the divine fullness as children of God.

Besides John and believers serving as witnesses to the Word becoming the Son in flesh, the narrator provides one more testimony to the incarnation: "The law indeed was given through Moses; grace and truth came through Jesus Christ" (1:17). What the text does is to contrast the law given "through Moses" with "grace and truth" that emanates from Jesus Christ. This statement—beginning with a conjunction in the Greek text, "for" (*hoti*), that functions with a causal force—helps to show, on the one hand, that Moses is an intermediate agent ("through Moses," *dia Mōuseōs*) to give God's law to the people, but, on the other hand, that grace and truth come from a different agent, namely, the Son of God ("through Jesus Christ," *Iēsou Christou*). Many traditional commentaries see the latter statement superseding the former statement. In other words, the text is conveying a contrast between Moses and Jesus Christ, with Jesus Christ replacing Moses and the law as the source of authority. However, one could also simply see this verse not so much as a contrast but simply as an additional statement about the fullness of God: God's boundless gift of both Moses/law and Jesus Christ/grace and truth. Nonetheless, the distinction between the intermediaries (Moses and Jesus Christ) in the text clearly shows the importance of accepting Jesus the Christ and the Word.

What is established is a dualistic construction of reality, with persons, ideas, traditions, and communities being classified by acceptance or rejection of Jesus Christ. This reality is communicated to others and then further enforced through the formation of an in-group or an out-group community.

Returning Home—The World Above: 1:18

The text takes one final turn. This time, it lifts its gaze to the world above once more. It is clear that to know God is not through sight but through Jesus's actions (grace) and words (truth). The final verse of this section emphasizes the invisibility of God: "No one has ever seen God. It is God the only Son, who is close to the Father's heart, who has made him known" (1:18). This emphasis of repeatedly not and never seeing God, as expressed through the iterative perfect ("seen," *heōraken*), surely points to God's mystery. According to the text, it is the only-begotten God (*monogenēs theou*) who reveals the mystery, that is, the Son who is chosen to reveal God's mystery to all. The Son has seen God (cf. 1:1b) and the Son has a special relationship with God (cf. 1:1c). He is so close that the Son is in the most affectionate relationship with the Father—he is close to the Father's heart or is in the bosom of the Father (*kolpon tou patros*). For this reason, the Son is chosen to reveal the mystery of God to the world; he is God and with God in the world above, God sends the only Son who takes on flesh in the world below to reveal God to all until he returns to the bosom of the Father. The prologue makes clear that the Son is divine and those who accept him as God's Son will be part of the children of God, and those who reject him will not be.

Conclusion

John's first division/narrative unit or prologue (1:1-18) is a text that envisions a dualistic worldview, with certain conceptualizations (priority, hierarchy, authority, and patriarchy) that draw lines between those who recognize (believe) and those who do not recognize (unbelief). The text gives the impression or suggestion that such division is "natural" and eternal, and this division now frames the rest of the story. Those who believe, therefore, are privileged for their belief: they are superior over others; they are more powerful than others; and they (men) are given opportunity over others. Such representation of a worldview with preexisting differences between the world, peoples, or places appears to be a placed-based version of the Word's journey to the world below. Westerners have since applied this version in the history of the "discovery" of the Americas to the detriment of many native and indigenous cultures. However, we should not create or impose walls between worlds, peoples, or places. For sure, Jn 1:1-18 presents a dualistic worldview perspective, which is understandable given the strong dualistic culture out of which John emerged. However, not challenging this dualistic view of reality suggests that such system is "natural" and divine. When the text itself questions this dualistic perspective with characters— such as the Samaritan woman, Mary and Martha, or the mother of Jesus— it acknowledges the possibility that something may be wrong with this perspective. Dualism only leads to a world split apart among its agents, actors, and subjects.

References

Jones, R. (2017), *Violent Borders: Refugees and the Right to Move*,
    London: Verso.
Segovia, F. F. (1991), "The Journey(s) of the Word: A Reading of the Plot of the
    Fourth Gospel," *Semeia* 53: 23–54.

Further Reading

Brown, R. E. (1966), *The Gospel According to John*, Anchor Bible 29,
    New York: Doubleday.
Culpepper, R. A. (1998), *The Gospel and Letters of John*, Interpreting Biblical
    Texts, Nashville, TN: Abingdon Press.
de Boer, M. C. (2015), "The Original Prologue to the Gospel of John," *NTS*
    61: 448–67.
Estes, D. (2015), "Rhetorical *Peristaseis* (Circumstances) in the Prologue of
    John," in K. B. Larsen (ed.), *The Gospel of John as Genre Mosaic*, Studia
    Aahusiana Neotestamentica 3, 191–208, Göttingen: Vandenhook &
    Ruprecht.
Moloney, F. J. (1993), *Belief in the Word: Reading John 1–4*, Philadelphia,
    PA: Fortress Press.
Segovia, F. F. (2002), "John 1:1–18 as Entrée into Johannine
    Reality: Representation and Ramifications," in J. Painter, R. A. Culpepper,
    and F. F. Segovia (eds.), *Word, Theology, and Community in John*, 33–64,
    St. Louis: Chalice Press.
Swanson, T. D. (2002), "To Prepare a Place: Johannine Christianity and the
    Collapse of Ethnic Territory," in M. W. Dube and J. L. Staley (eds.), *John and
    Postcolonialism: Travel, Space and Power*, The Bible and Postcolonialism, 7,
    11–50, Sheffield: Sheffield Academic Press.

5

John 17:1-26: A Prayer for Unity and Community

Chapter Outline

Introduction 86
Jesus Prays for Himself (17:1-5) 87
Jesus Prays for His Disciples (17:6-19) 89
Jesus Prays for All Believers (17:20-26) 92
Conclusion 94
Further Reading 96

Although the last chapter dealt with Jn 1:1-18 and its dualistic construction of reality at the beginning of John, such construction holds true toward the end of the Gospel as well with the final prayer by Jesus (17:1-26). As with 1:1-18, attention to the pretextual history of the prayer is suspended not because it is not vital, but because a choice to focus on the narrative itself and the cultural world it advances provides a different angle to look at this prayer. The prayer is a moment at the end of the second division (narrative of travel/crossing) that connects the human with the divine. Such a moment is important to examine, for it reveals the vision of John for the future.

Introduction

It can be argued that Jesus's final prayer serves as a summary of the Gospel as a whole: the Father has sent the Son into an unbelieving world to bring unbelievers to God, so that unbelievers may experience the same love that God has bestowed upon the Son through the Son's self-sacrifice of himself before an unbelieving world. The prayer comes at the end of the farewell address (13:1–17:26) in which Jesus explains the meaning of his impending ordeal (arrest, death, and resurrection) and of the ordeal that his disciples and believers will experience when he returns to the world above. The prayer thus functions as a final appeal to God for unity among believers (including but also not limited to the disciples in John). This unity prepares all of Jesus's followers to endure the unbelieving world after Jesus's departure and protects them against this unbelieving world. Jesus, in the presence of God, seeks God's will for unity, which is an essential part of what it means to be a member of the Johannine community. This unity is dependent upon his unity with the Father (17:1-5), unity of the disciples (17:6-9), and unity of all believers (17:20-26).

In the Fourth Gospel, this theological theme of unity is the basis for community. The prayer, as we will see, evokes a sense of community that calls for a sense of belonging, shared vision, and mutual trust. A consequence of such an emphasis on community is that it always excludes. While community, on the one hand, is based on shared beliefs and a secure way of life, it, on the other hand, often encourages the building of a wall that separates "us" from "them" and leads to intolerant portrayals of others outside this community. In what follows, I will keep in mind this potential problem of (over)emphasizing unity and perform a reading of the prayer in a literary–ideological perspective. As mentioned above, this is not to say that the social–historical world of the text is not significant, but rather that this reading simply focuses on the prayer as a literary (or narrative) and ideological product. Many commentaries on John provide helpful information about the prayer's historical and theological background, but my focus is more attuned to how such a prayer functions as a literary and ideological expression on community. For sure, all literary texts are ideological in the sense that they are expressing ideas to someone else, but here ideological signifies the many ways meaning serves relations of domination or power. Such a reading of the prayer remains informed, of course, by other studies, particularly Johannine literary studies.

The prayer comes at an important juncture in the plot of the story: between Jesus's address to his disciples with special instructions before his departure (13:31–16:33) and the "hour" when Jesus gives himself up to the authorities so that the disciples may join him in the world above (18:1–20:25). In its quest for unity or its pursuit for a solidified community of believers, the prayer sets in motion, with proleptic language foreshadowing the story of the early Christian movement, the setting apart (or sanctification) of the disciples (and believers) from the world below. To secure this vision of the community, Jesus prays for (1) himself (17:1-5), (2) his disciples (17:6-19), and (3) all believers (17:20-26).

Jesus Prays for Himself (17:1-5)

Before Jesus actually begins the prayer proper, the narrator provides two brief introductory remarks: first, the narrator references the farewell address (13:31–16:33) to establish when Jesus actually says the prayer in story time ("After Jesus had spoken these words," 17:1a); second, the narrator describes Jesus's posture during the prayer ("he looked up to heaven and said," 17:1b). Both of these remarks establish the importance of the prayer by way of its placement in the story, but they also detail Jesus's respectful posture toward God the Father as he turns his gaze away from the world below toward the world above.

The prayer proper begins with Jesus addressing God as "Father" (*pater*, 17:1c). Such reference to God recurs in 17:5, 21, 24 and with modifiers in 17:11 ("holy Father") and 17:25 ("righteous Father"), thus reinforcing a patriarchal representation of God and a hierarchical structure of the universe. Such beginning shows God the Father to be above all, both physically and spiritually. What follows is Jesus alerting God that the time ("the hour") has come—that is, the hour pointing to Jesus's death and resurrection has at last arrived—and the current age is ushered in place of a new age (17:1d; cf. 2:4; 7:6, 8; 8:20; 12:23, 27, 31; 13:1, 31). Because the hour has come, Jesus beseeches the Father to glorify the Son as the Son glorifies the Father (17:1e). It is at this point that the prayer turns to Jesus himself. Jesus's first request calls on God to honor him as he has honored the Father. This mutual glorification, a glorification also called upon at the beginning of the farewell address (13:31), summarizes in a way the whole prayer. Jesus's first petition for God is to be empowered, thus establishing Jesus's authority (*exousian*) over all (17:2a). This authorizes Jesus to provide eternal life to all those whom the Father has called to Jesus (17:2b). Jesus insinuates here that some are selected as believers of God and some are not; the verse is therefore suggestive of an in-group of believers and an out-group of unbelievers. In other words, those who know Jesus, the Son, knows the Father (17:2-3). Knowing (*ginōskōsin*) here does not only imply intellectual knowledge, it also suggests believing. Knowing the Father through the Son means that believers know that the Father has sent Jesus Christ (*Iēsoun Christon*), through whom God is known. Sharing in eternal life with the Son/Father solidifies unity among all (Father/Son/believers) in the world above well into eternity. Thus, a notion of a closed community of believers is surely set against a community of unbelievers.

Continuing to pray to the Father on his own behalf, Jesus changes from the third person to the first person in referring to himself: "I glorified you on earth by finishing the work that you gave me to do" (17:4). Jesus emphatically ("I" [*egō*]) wants to reaffirm that he has glorified God ("you" [*se*]) in the world below. Jesus has fulfilled the mission he was sent to do ("I glorified [*edoxasa*] you on earth," 17:4a). He was sent to do the work of the Father and he has completed it. Such work honors the Father. As a result, Jesus addresses the Father directly once more: "So now, Father, glorify me in your own presence with the glory that I had in your presence before the world existed" (17:5). The adverb "now" (*nyn*) indicates that an important point is to come; this is reinforced with Jesus addressing the Father once more directly ("Father" [*pater*]). He clarifies that his request is to experience once more the Father's presence and glory at the Father's side as he did before creation ("in your presence before the world existed," 17:5c). He is praying to the Father, since his earthly mission is finished, that he may return to his resumed place next to the Father (cf. 1:1). This request is again built on a mutual or reciprocal glorification between the Son and the Father that evokes a notion of unity to be extended to the community of believers.

In sum, the first five verses focus on Jesus praying on behalf of himself. He makes two points: first, with the authority given to him by his Father, he has completed his mission to bring eternal life to believers (17:1-3); second, Jesus asks the Father to glorify him just as he has glorified the Father through his own sacrifice or "finishing [of] the work" (17:4-5). In short, he prays that the mutual relationship that exists between him and the Father will be reflected in the unity among his believers. It is a call, in some way, for a new world (above?) in which all those who believe shall receive eternal life and be a part of a community united in the oneness of the Father and Son.

Jesus Prays for His Disciples (17:6-19)

The prayer now focuses on the disciples; they will now serve as the subject of Jesus's prayer and will be the main topic of the prayer until 17:19: "I have made your name known to those [*tois anthrōpois*] whom you gave me from the world, they were yours, and you gave them to me, and they have kept your word" (17:6). The disciples, who were given by the Father to the Son, are "from the world" (17:6a, cf. 17:2b)—that is, they are from the world below, yet they are not "of the world" because they believe in the Son. As disciples, Jesus reminds the Father, they have remained obedient and have kept their promise to proclaim the word of God. The disciples' obedience signals that they are protectors and transmitters of Jesus's manifestation of God through their teachings of the Word. They are the expression of the work or the completed work of the Father and the Son.

The disciples are fully aware of the source of Jesus's work. They know (*egnōkan*) or "they have come to know" that all that Jesus has expressed through his words and actions comes from God. Throughout the plot of the Gospel, Jesus has given the disciples his revelation and they have come to recognize or believe that God sent Jesus, God's only Son, to them so that they may accept Jesus's words (*ta rhēmata*) and know/believe with certainty Jesus's relationship with the Father (17:7-8). By knowing (v. 7) and believing (v. 8) that Jesus came from God and was sent by God, the disciples become a community; their sense of belonging is established around a shared belief.

Jesus emphatically ("I" [*egō*]) is "asking" (*erōtō*) or praying to the Father for the disciples ("their" [*autōn*]). In doing so, Jesus is not praying for the world below (i.e., unbelievers) because the world below is not the Father's. Rather, Jesus prays for the disciples because the disciples are part of the Father's (and the Son's) community: "because they are yours" (17:9d). In creating such a community, the consequence is the breeding of an "other"; in this case, it is the world below, despite Jesus's earlier claim to save the world (cf. 3:16). The world is surely represented as the place where many people do not know and do not believe in the Son, but the disciples are the Father's ("they are yours" [*soi eisin*], 17:9d). Just as Jesus's disciples are the Father's, the Father's chosen ones are Jesus's. Ownership of the disciples is thus also mutual (17:10a-b); as a result of this reciprocal relationship between the Father and the Son, the disciples' belief in the Son, and mutual ownership of the disciples by the

Father and the Son, Jesus is made known and glorified. The disciples, for whom Jesus is ardently praying, are the ones who will take Jesus's words and mission to the unbelieving world below. The disciples are the transmitters of his message, and for this reason, Jesus petitions the Father that the disciples, who are of the world, be considered "special" or "privileged," for their role is to fulfill the mission of Jesus to the unbelieving world (17:11a-c).

Jesus speaks to the Father majestically ("holy Father" [*pater hagie*]), entreating the Father not only to protect the disciples but also to unite them as one (17:11d-e). The prayer aims to unite the disciples so that its community may continue to be one (*hina ōsin hen*, 17:11f), as the Father and the Son are one (17:11g). The purpose of the prayer appears to be the Father's protection of the disciples against the world. In other words, the unity and hence community of the disciples or believers is born out of not only the shared belief of the community in the Father and Son but also fear, which manifests itself by casting the world below as hostile and dangerous to the disciples and their mission to the world. Fear, it can be argued, is the impetus for the prayer. The demand to be faithful also calls on the faithful to be fearful of its enemies, thus creating an "us"-versus-"them" mentality. Unity and community may seem harmonious, but, as shown by Jesus's prayer, they also cause division.

Just as Jesus protected the disciples against the world during his ministry, despite losing one (i.e., Judas), Jesus calls on the Father to do the same after he returns to the Father: "While I was with them, I protected them in your name, and not one of them was lost except the one destined to be lost, so that the scripture might be fulfilled" (17:12). Jesus prays to the Father to "protect" (*etēroun*) and "guard" (*ephulaxa*) the disciples from the community of unbelievers, with which "the one destined to be lost," or literally "the son of the lost or of perdition" (*ho huios tēs apōleias*), chose to associate—supposedly in accordance to scripture (cf. Ps 41:9). Jesus prays, therefore, for unity, because unity will empower the disciples against those like "the son of perdition." Thus, in calling on the Father—out of fear—to keep them safe while in the world, the prayer also conveys a dualistic mindset: a community of believers and its necessary "other," a community of unbelievers.

Still focused on the disciples, Jesus "now" (*nyn*), a temporal designation, affirms that he is returning to the Father (13:1a) and explains that he "speaks these things" (*tauta lalō*)—that is, talking out loud—for a purpose. Not only does Jesus pray that the disciples will be protected and united (17:11-12), Jesus is also petitioning the Father that they may experience the very "joy" (*tēn charan*) that he himself experiences in his relationship with the Father

(17:13b). Joy, a deep euphoric emotion (cf. 15:11; 16:22, 24), allows the disciples to experience the same blissful experience that Jesus has experienced with the Father. Along with joy, Jesus prays for protection and unity, all ideas related to the notion of community. Protection keeps outsiders from harming the community, unity maintains believers' cohesiveness in the face of outsiders, and joy allows them to experience peace in or among themselves.

This sense of community comes out further in the prayer when Jesus, still speaking on behalf of the disciples, explains to the Father the consequences of being members of a community (17:14a). Jesus tells the Father that he has imparted the Father's Word to the disciples. The disciples will continue to have this Word in the present (*egō dedōka*), "and" (*kai*)—adding more information—the world has begun to hate them (*ho kosmos emisēsen autous*).

The reason for such hate of the disciples is because they are no longer members of the world below (14:14b) in the same way that Jesus is not part of the world below. In other words, the disciples are not of the unbelieving world and, because of that, the world does not see them as part of their community, just as it does not include Jesus within its world. Again, the prayer is projecting a dualistic worldview. From the point of view of the prayer, the communal solidarity of the believing world is just as united as the communal solidarity of the unbelieving world. Both communities manifest outright rejection and even hatred for the other.

Jesus qualifies his request by conveying to the Father that he is not calling for the disciples to leave the world below, but rather that they remain among the unbelievers (17:15a). If they were to be removed from the world below, as the prayer insinuates, it would mean that they would follow Jesus to the world above. Another way of understanding Jesus's statement is that though the disciples are not part of the sphere of the unbelieving world, they have a mission to this unbelieving world. Perhaps this is why Jesus once again petitions the Father "to protect them from the evil one" (*tērēsēs autous ek tou ponērou*). Jesus does not just ask softly, he—through the use of the adversative "but" (*alla*)—entreats the Father to act against "the evil one" (*ponērou*). And the reason why, as he reiterates the rationale already expressed in 17:14, is because the disciples "do not belong to the world, just as I do not belong to the world" (17:16). Thus, Jesus is petitioning the Father to protect the disciples while they are in the world below. They are the target of "the evil one" and, out of this sense of fear and danger, Jesus beseeches the Father to protect them. Again, it is out of this fear and danger that a community is forming—a community that is based (partly) on, depending on one's viewpoint, a one-way or mutual hatred. This is the reason for such a call for protection.

To protect them, Jesus entreats the Father to "sanctify" (*hagiason*) the disciples (17:17a). He is calling on the Father to set them apart or make them holy from the world for their mission (cf. 10:36). They should be sanctified "in (or by) the truth" (*en tē alētheia*) to carry on the word of God. Such sanctification through the truth of the Word will protect them. With a declarative statement, Jesus confirms that the Father's word is truth: "Sanctify them in the truth; your word is truth" (17:17).

Because of their lack of belonging in this world, Jesus asks the Father to set the disciples apart for their divinely sanctioned mission (17:18). Jesus, with a comparative clause ("As you have sent me into the world," 17:18a), expresses that he was given a mission to go to the world and, as a result ("so I" or "and I" [*kagō*]), Jesus commissions the disciples to go to the world. Such commissioning is a reason why they need blessing as well as protection. They are called to establish a community in the world—a community that will bring unbelievers to the Father as believers.

As Jesus prays for the disciples' protection, he expresses his willingness to sanctify himself (*kai hyper autōn egō hagiazō emauton*, 17:19a) for the benefit of the disciples. He does so (sanctifies himself) in order that they themselves may be set apart in truth, repeating the expression in 17:17. In other words, by sanctifying himself, Jesus makes it possible for them to be sanctified or making it possible for them to be sent out into the world to bring believers to him.

In praying for the welfare of his disciples (17:6-19), Jesus paves the way for the disciples to continue existing as a community, a body of believers in the world below and through whom Jesus Christ (17:3) works in the world. This unified community, reflected in the unity of the Father and the Son, is necessary to endure "the evil one" or unbelievers. At the same time, another community is forming and it comprises of unbelievers. These outsiders or unbelievers are being characterized as evil. Prayer can at times, as 17:6-19 suggests, petition for protection against evil forces, but, ironically, it also can construct the "evil other," as it does here.

Jesus Prays for All Believers (17:20-26)

Jesus now shifts his focus and prays for all those who will become believers through the disciples' word (17:20). The scope of the prayer widens: it moves from Jesus himself (17:1-5) to the disciples (17:6-19), and now to all believers (17:20-26). He prays that, through their faith, they will all be in unity: "I ask not only on behalf of these, but also on behalf of those who will believe in me through their word, that they may all be one" (17:20-21a). Having prayed for the unity of the disciples (17:11), Jesus now petitions the Father that all believers will be united, just as he and the Father are one (17:20b-d). But Jesus takes it further and prays that these believers are also "in us" (*en hēmin*)—that is, they too will be united with the Father and Son. Jesus is concerned that the believers remain as one—not as some other community but rather a community that is "in" them. In other words, he wants a community that reflects the unity of the Father and the Son: "As you, Father, are in me and I am in you, may they also be in us, so that the world may believe that you have sent me" (17:21b-e). Jesus's reason for this particular petition is his desire for future believers in the unbelieving world to show to this world that Jesus is indeed God's emissary (17:21f). The unbelieving world does not believe that the Father has sent the Son, so Jesus prays that his believers' show of unity will lead to belief in Jesus's unity with the Father and hence his identity as one who is sent from the world above. For Jesus, all believers must remain unified as followers of Jesus Christ the Son if they are to endure the unbelieving world. Unity as a community of believers (in the Father and the Son) not only protects them but also exhibits the truth of Jesus's word.

This theme of unity continues in Jesus's prayer. As before (17:4-5), Jesus speaks to God about the glory that he shares with the Father: Jesus has extended this glory (*doxan*), this honor, to his believers for the purpose (*hina ōsin*) that they will be one, just as the Father and the Son are one (17:22). As Jesus departs, he prays to the Father that the Father and the Son come to dwell with the believers. This dwelling ("I in them and you in me," 17:23a) is for the purpose (*hina*) that they "become completely one" (*teteleiōmenoi eis*, 17:23b). Unity is thus an essential part of the Johannine community. Jesus desires this unity "so that" (*hina*, 17:23c) the world knows that Jesus was sent from God and that God loves these believers just as God has loved the Son (17:23c). Moreover, without unity, believers will become vulnerable in this unbelieving world; this is the fear that is expressed in Jesus's prayer.

As a response to this fear, Jesus addresses God as Father once more and implores the Father with his desire (*thelō*) that those believers who have been sent to Jesus share with him a place in the world above: "Father, I desire that those also, whom you have given me, may be with me where I am, to see my glory, which you have given me because you loved me before the foundation of the world" (17:24). Only in this sharing can these believers see his glory, which the Father has given to him through the Father's love manifested across the world (*pro katabolēs kosmou*, 17:24e).

In his concluding words in the prayer, Jesus provides an epithet that points to God's ethical character: "'Righteous' (*dikaie*) Father, the world does not know you, but I know you; and these know that you have sent me" (17:25). This address of God, as "Righteous Father," points to Jesus's appeal to the Father's notion of justice. Jesus appeals to God's character of justice because he knows that the world has failed to recognize God as Jesus's Father (17:25b), and he knows that a just God will not abandon the believers. At the same time, Jesus does know the Father and his believers know Jesus's identity as God's emissary (17:25c-d), because these believers, unlike unbelievers, have known or "know" (*egnōsan*) that God is a righteous God (17:25b). Having made God known (*egnōrisa*) to his believers (*autois*) in the past, Jesus will continue to make God known (*gnōrisō*) in the future: "I made your name known to them, and I will make it known, so that the love with which you have loved me may be in them, and I in them" (17:26). The reason why he will make God known is expressed through a purpose clause (*hina*); it has to do with love (*agapē*). The love that the Father has given the Son is given as well to believers, just as the love of the Son is given to them (*en autois*). To put it another way, God's love in the believers and the Son's love in them are what unify the Johannine community. Jesus finishes the prayer to the Father with this theme of love: the love of God and of the Son manifesting itself through community.

Conclusion

The final prayer of Jesus summarizes many important Johannine ideas of the Gospel: glory, love, determinism, faith, the world, and believers/unbelievers. One theme that is also present is the concept of community. The prayer functions, among other things, to not only reinforce a community's identity but also set it apart from other communities such as the unbelieving world. Jesus, the disciples, and the believers all represent a distinct community that is separate from the unbelieving world. This perspective is based in part on John's dualistic worldview, which casts the world below as an unbelieving, hostile place. As 17:16 suggests, neither Jesus nor his followers belong to this world. The prayer emphasizes, therefore, Jesus's and his community's struggles to establish an identity through "othering": a world of believers against a world of unbelievers. Because of this unbelieving world, Jesus turns, right before his impending trial and death, to the Father in prayer for his believers' protection (17:15) as they embark on their mission to the world. This community's mission is to make Jesus known and to manifest Jesus's love through belief in the Father. Jesus is not praying that believers escape from the world below. Rather, he prays that they will not conform to the world, that they will be protected from the hatred in the world, and that they will remain steadfast in their mission to reveal the revelation of Jesus to unbelievers and bring them to Jesus. Their mission is to reflect the love of Jesus in their relationship with fellow believers.

This new community is to be united, in the model of the unity that exists between the Father and the Son, in order to protect believers from the unbelieving world. When the world sees this unity, they will come to recognize Jesus as all believers do. All those who believe will possess the knowledge or recognition of Jesus, while Jesus continues to make the love of God known. The prayer projects an image of an inclusive and harmonious community covered with the love of God but set against the world.

There is, therefore, another side of community that needs closer scrutiny. If [a] community projects belonging and unity, it also has an underside that often promotes exclusion and oppression. Community, as constructed in the final prayer of Jesus, is one that is built upon a specific kind of social stratification (believers over unbelievers) and embedded in patriarchal social relations (Father and Son). Acceptance within the community is based on whether one is a believer or not; believers think of themselves as chosen or authentic, while all others are excluded. As a result, we have a bifurcated social world with those who belong to the world above (believers) against those who exist in the world below (unbelievers). For some, this notion of a close and closed community, as reflected in the prayer, is still legitimate and valid: what you believe or your way of life is understood to be above or superior to other beliefs or ways of life. An alternative path is to build different but equal communities, a path that allows communities to connect across the globe. It is in this latter notion of an open community that I see God at work in the entire world; mine is a God who values right relationships over correct beliefs.

Jesus speaks to God through prayer. It is through prayer that believers also talk to God, whether it is to glorify God, thank God, or ask God for blessings, comfort, forgiveness, and even protection against evil. There are many reasons why one prays in the world today, privately and publicly. However, solemn prayers—even those for unity within—do not necessarily serve the cause of unity and harmony in the world. What really serves such a cause is a shared vision of love that promotes openness rather than opposition toward difference.

Further Reading

Brown, R. E. (1966), *The Gospel According to John*, Anchor Bible 29, New York: Doubleday.

Culpepper, R. A. (1998), *The Gospel and Letters of John*, Interpreting Biblical Texts, Nashville, TN: Abingdon Press.

Moloney, F. J. (1998), *Glory Not Dishonor: Reading John 13–21*, Minneapolis, MN: Fortress Press.

Segovia, F. F. (1998), "Inclusion and Exclusion in John 17: An Intercultural Reading," in F. F. Segovia (ed.), *"What Is John?", Vol. II, Literary and Social Readings of the Fourth Gospel*, Symposium Series, 281–322, Atlanta: Society of Biblical Literature.

Conclusion:
John, the "Maverick"
Gospel—Revisited

The Gospel of John is certainly a "maverick" Gospel, as Robert Kysar so succinctly put it in 1976 (Kysar 2007). "Maverick" draws on the Western trope of a loner who does things "his" own way. As Kysar suggests, John is a nonconformist Gospel compared to the Synoptic Gospels, where much of the material is similar or parallel to one another. John is doing things "his" own way, in "his" own voice, and according to "his" own identity, context, and understanding (historical, literary, theological). It does provide a different reading experience from the Synoptics. But the Western trope, "maverick," can also mean something different depending on the point of view of the reader. A "maverick" can be viewed not as an independent, nonconformist, free thinker; it can also be viewed as a trespasser, occupier, or colonizer. For many who live in what has been called the Southwest borderlands between or near the US/Mexico border (i.e., Mexicans, Mexican-Americans, and Native Americans), a "maverick," signifying an "Anglo-American," is not a nonconformist. Instead, it means a version or copy of those in history who thought that they had discovered "America" but in reality had conquered and occupied a land that was already inhabited by other people. The same can also be said of Christopher Columbus, who supposedly "discovered" the Americas in 1492, but in fact stumbled across it or, from a postcolonial perspective, conquered it. Is John really a "maverick" Gospel with an independent voice against the dominant world? Or is John simply a zealous Gospel hidden with a superior mindset to convert others? Or is it a bit of both?

As I discussed in Chapter 1, how one narrates a story depends on the person and the process that is involved in telling the story. This will contribute to how one sees or approaches John. That is, the process of writing about "what happened" (narrative of facts) is different from writing about "that which is said to have happened" (narrativization of story) for both sociohistorical and literary interpreters. While the former tries her or his best to focus on approximating the past without discussing the present, the latter focuses on the process of historical or literary production or narrativization in relation to the present. Of course, knowingly or not, the past is always written from the present.

It is the overlap of these two hermeneutical positions that may help Johannine interpreters make further and better sense of the story of John. By critically studying the overlap between the sociohistorical world of John (what was said to have happened) and the narrativization of this world (that which is said to have happened), one sees both the power and the ambiguity of the story. What one receives when such positions are intertwined is a Johannine story interpreted from a certain point of view. The texts as well as their interpretations are simply constructions. If history is about "what happened," why don't all historical or literary interpretations of John tell the same history (or story)? It is not just about "what happened," it is also about "that which is said to have happened"; both are always already informed by the subjectivity of the interpreter.

John, the "maverick" Gospel, is a story infused with power. Reading John as a single moment of history (e.g., a two-level drama approach as discussed in Chapter 1) accommodates Sunday-school teachers, preachers, professors, and publishers who sell the story in cleverly crafted rhetoric or in nicely bounded books for immediate consumption. Such packaging of history avoids any thinking about power and any thinking about how "what happened" overlaps with "that which is said to have happened." If the history of the Mayflower or the Battle of the Alamo becomes the center of "what happened," one could understand why a maverick cowboy is perceived (as in Hollywood Westerns such as "Battle of the Alamo") as an independent and nonconformist who overcomes "hostiles." But imagine if US history begins with the story of immigration or with inhabitants of the borderlands, such history would perhaps not reduce immigrants or the inhabitants of the borderlands to "visitors" or potential "intruders." In my reading of John above, I continue to see John as a "maverick" Gospel, but a "maverick" Gospel with multiple stories and various pasts. The ideological approach that I embraced in this reading of John aims modestly to bring such stories and pasts to the forefront. To put it differently, this reading of John aims to bring to the forefront those voices that have been silenced by years of readings that see John through a singular and one-sided history. Such readings of John and of history, just like the dominant versions of US history or Southwest borderlands history have done, influence how we see the "other" as hostile and evil enemies (unbelievers) rather than as human beings. I read John to bring forth different voices in and about the story, including those that are problematic and possibly harmful, so we can develop a better vision for everyone in our world.

Bibliography

Appleby, Joyce, Lynn Hunt, and Margaret Jacob. *Telling the Truth about History*. New York: W. W. Norton, 1994.

Ashton, John A. *Understanding the Fourth Gospel*. Oxford: Clarendon Press, 1991.

Bauman, Zygmunt. *Legislators and Interpreters*. Cambridge: Polity Press, 1987.

Benko, Andrew G. "Race in John: Racializing Discourse in the Fourth Gospel." PhD diss., Brite Divinity School, 2018.

Bennema, Cornelis. "A Comprehensive Approach to Understanding Character in the Gospel of John." In *Characters and Characterization in the Gospel of John*, Library of New Testament Studies 461, edited by Christopher W. Skinner, 36–58. New York: T&T Clark, 2013.

Bennema, Cornelis. *Encountering Jesus: Character Studies in the Gospel of John*, 2nd ed. Minneapolis, MN: Fortress Press, 2014.

Brown, Raymond E. *The Gospel According to John*, 2 vols. Anchor Bible 29-29A. New York: Doubleday, 1966–70.

Brown, Raymond E. *The Community of the Beloved Disciple*. New York: Paulist Press, 1979.

Brown, Sherri, and Christopher W. Skinner (eds.). *Johannine Ethics: The Moral World of the Gospel and Epistle of John*. Minneapolis, MN: Fortress Press, 2017.

Bryant, Jo-Ann A. *John*. Grand Rapids, MI: Baker, 2011.

Bultmann, Rudolf. *The Gospel of John: A Commentary*. Translated by G. R. Beasley-Murray, R. W. N. Hoare, and J. K. Riches. Philadelphia, PA: Westminster, 1971.

Callahan, Allen Dwight. "John." In *True to Our Native Land: An African American New Testament Commentary*, edited by Brian K. Blount, 186–212. Minneapolis, MN: Fortress Press, 2007.

Carter, Warren. *John and Empire: Initial Explorations*. New York: T&T Clark, 2008.

Castles, Stephen, and Mark. J. Miller (eds.). *The Age of Migration: International Population Movements in the Modern World*, 4th ed. New York: Guilford Press, 2009.

Cohen, Shaye J. D. *The Beginnings of Jewishness: Boundaries, Varieties, Uncertainties*. Berkeley: University of California Press, 1999.

Conway, Colleen M. *Men and Women in the Fourth Gospel: Gender and Johannine Characterization.* SBL Dissertation Series 167. Atlanta: Society of Biblical Literature, 1999.

Conway, Colleen M. "Speaking through Ambiguity: Minor Characters in the Fourth Gospel." *Biblical Interpretation* 10 (2002): 324–41.

Culpepper, R. Alan. *The Johannine School,* SBL Dissertation Series, 26. Missoula: Scholars, 1975.

Culpepper, R. Alan. *Anatomy of the Fourth Gospel: A Study in Literary Design.* Philadelphia, PA: Fortress Press, 1983.

Culpepper, R. Alan. *The Gospel and Letters of John.* Nashville, TN: Abingdon, 1998.

De Boer, Martinus C. "The Original Prologue to the Gospel of John." *New Testament Studies* 61 (2015): 448–67.

Dube, Musa W. "Reading for Decolonization (John 4:1-42)." *Semeia* 75 (1996): 37–59.

Dube, Musa W. *Postcolonial Feminist Interpretation of the Bible.* St. Louis: Chalice Press, 2000.

Dube, Musa W., and Jeffrey L. Staley (eds.). *John and Postcolonialism: Travel, Space and Power.* The Bible and Postcolonialism, 7. Sheffield: Sheffield Academic Press, 2002.

Estes, Douglas. *The Temporal Mechanics of the Fourth Gospel: A Theory of Hermeneutical Relativity in the Gospel of John.* Leiden: Brill, 2008.

Fehribach, Adeline. *The Women in the Life of the Bridegroom: A Feminist Historical-Literary Analysis of the Female Characters in the Fourth Gospel.* Collegeville: Liturgical Press, 1998.

Fraser, Nancy, and Axel Honneth. *Redistribution or Recognition? A Political-Philosophical Exchange.* London: Verso, 2003.

Gadamer, Hans-Georg. *Truth and Method.* Translated by William Glen-Doepel. Edited by John Cumming and Garrett Barden, 2nd ed. London: Sheed and Ward, 1979.

Goss, Robert E. "John." In *The Queer Bible Commentary*, edited by Deryn Guest, Robert E. Goss, and Mona West, 548–65. London: SCM, 2006.

Guardiola-Sáenz, Letica A. "Border-crossing and Its Redemptive Power in John 7.53–8.11: A Cultural Reading of Jesus and the *Accused*." In *John and Postcolonialism: Travel, Space and Power.* The Bible and Postcolonialism, 7, edited by Musa W. Dube and Jeffrey L. Staley, 129–52. Sheffield: Sheffield Academic Press, 2002.

Gundry, Robert. H. *A Survey of the New Testament*, 4th ed. Grand Rapids, MI: Zondervan, 2003.

Hengel, Martin. *The Johannine Question.* Translated by J. Bowden. Philadelphia, PA: Trinity Press International, 1990.

Hylen, Susan E. *Imperfect Believers: Ambiguous Characters in the Gospel of John*. Louisville, KY: Westminster John Knox Press, 2009.

Interpretation: A Journal of Bible and Theology (The Gospel of John), vol. XLIX (4) (October 1995): 341–89.

Jeanrond, Werner. *Theological Hermeneutics*. London: SCM Press, 1994.

Keener, Craig. S. *The Gospel of John: A Commentary*, 2 vols. Peabody, MA: Hendrickson, 2003.

Kim, Jean Kim. *Woman and Nation: An Intercontextual Reading of the Gospel of John from a Postcolonial Feminist Perspective*. Leiden: Brill, 2004.

Köstenberger, Andreas J. *John*. Baker Exegetical Commentary on the New Testament. Grand Rapids, MI: Baker, 2004.

Kysar, Robert. *John's Story of Jesus*. Philadelphia, PA: Fortress Press, 1984.

Kysar, Robert. *John: The Maverick Gospel*, 3rd ed. Louisville, KY: Westminster John Knox Press, 2007.

Kwok, Pui-lan, *Discovering the Bible in the Non-Biblical World*. Maryknoll, NY: Orbis Books, 1995.

Liew, Tat-Siong Benny. "Ambiguous Admittance: Consent and Descent in John's Community of 'Upward' Mobility." In *John and Postcolonialism: Travel, Space and Power*. The Bible and Postcolonialism, 7, edited by Musa. W. Dube and Jeffrey Staley, 193–224. Sheffield: Sheffield Academic Press. 2002.

Lozada Jr., Francisco. "Contesting an Interpretation of John 5: Moving Beyond Colonial Evangelism." In *John and Postcolonialism: Travel, Space and Power*. The Bible and Postcolonialism, 7, edited by Musa. W. Dube and Jeffrey Staley, 76–93. Sheffield: Sheffield Academic Press. 2002.

Lozada Jr., Francisco "Social Location and Johannine Scholarship: Looking Ahead." In *New Currents through John: A Global Perspective*, edited by Francisco Lozada Jr. and Tom Thatcher, 183–97. Atlanta: Society of Biblical Literature, 2006.

Lozada Jr., Francisco. "Teaching the New Testament: Toward an Expanded Contextual Approach." In *Soundings in Cultural Criticism: Perspectives and Methods in Culture, Power, and Identity in the New Testament*, edited by Francisco Lozada Jr. and Greg Carey, 151–64. Minneapolis, MN: Fortress Press, 2013.

Lozada Jr., Francisco. "Narrative Identities of the Gospel of John." In *The Oxford Handbook to Biblical Narrative*, edited by Dana Nolan Fewel, 341–50. Oxford: Oxford University Press, 2016.

Lozada Jr., Francisco. *Toward a Latino/a Biblical Interpretation*. Atlanta: SBL Publications, 2017.

Lozada Jr., Francisco, and Tom Thatcher (eds.). *New Currents through John: A Global Perspective*. Atlanta: Society of Biblical Literature, 2006.

Martínez, Oscar J. *Border People: Life and Society in the U.S.–Mexico Borderlands*. Arizona: University of Arizona Press, 1994.

Martyn, J. Louis. *History and Theology in the Fourth Gospel*, 2nd ed. Nashville, TN: Abingdon Press, 1979.

Miller, J. Maxwell. "Reading the Bible Historically: The Historian's Approach." In *To Each Its Own Meaning: An Introduction to Biblical Criticism and Their Application*, edited by Steven L. McKenzie and Stephen R. Haynes, 11–28. Louisville, KY: Westminster John Knox Press.

Moloney, Francis J. *Belief in the Word: Reading John 1–4*. Minneapolis, MN: Fortress Press, 1993.

Moloney, Francis J. *Signs and Shadows: Reading John 5-12*. Minneapolis, MN: Fortress Press, 1996.

Moloney, Francis J. *Glory Not Dishonor: Reading John 13-21*. Minneapolis, MN: Fortress Press, 1998.

Myers, Alicia D. *Characterizing Jesus: A Rhetorical Analysis on the Fourth Gospel's Use of Scripture in Its Presentation of Jesus*. Library of New Testament Studies 458. New York: T&T Clark, 2014.

Myers, Alicia D. "Just Opponents? Ambiguity, Empathy, and the Jews in the Gospel of John." In *Johannine Ethics: The Moral World of the Gospel and Epistles of John*, edited by Sherri Brown and Christopher W. Skinner, 159–76. Minneapolis, MN: Fortress Press, 2017.

O'Day, Gail. "The Gospel of John." In *New Interpreter's Bible*, vol. 9, edited by Leander E. Keck, 491–865. Nashville, TN: Abingdon Press, 1995.

Okure, Teresa. *The Johannine Approach to Mission: A Contextual Study of John 4:1-42*. Wissenschafliche Untersuchungen zum Neuen Tetament 2/31. Tübingen: Mohr Siebeck, 1988.

Painter, John, R. Alan Culpepper, and Fernando F. Segovia (eds.). *Word, Theology, and Community in John*. St. Louis: Chalice Press, 2002.

Palmer, Richard E. *Hermeneutics: Interpretation Theory in Schleiermacher, Dilthey, Heidegger, and Gadamer*. Evanston, IL: Northwestern University Press, 1969.

Powell, Mark Allan. *The Gospels*. Minneapolis, MN: Fortress Press, 1998.

Reinhartz, Adele. "The Gospel of John." In *Searching the Scriptures*, vol. II, edited by Elisabeth Schüssler Fiorenza, 561–634. New York: Crossroad, 1994.

Reinhartz, Adele. "The Johannine Community and Its Jewish Neighbors." In *"What Is John?" Volume II, Literary and Social Readings of the Fourth Gospel*, edited by Fernando F. Segovia, 111–38. Atlanta: Society of Biblical Literature, 1998.

Reinhartz, Adele. *Befriending the Beloved Disciple*. New York: Continuum, 2001.

Resseguie, James L. *The Strange Gospel: Narrative Design & Point of View.* Leiden: Brill, 2001.

Schnackenburg, Rudolf. *The Gospel According to St. John*, 3 vols. Translated by Kevin Smyth. New York: Seabury. 1968–1982.

Schneiders, Sandra M. *Written That You May Believe: Encountering Jesus in the Fourth Gospel.* New York: Crossroad, 1999.

Schüssler-Fiorenza, Elisabeth. *In Memory of Her: A Feminist-Theological Reconstruction of Christian Origins.* New York: Crossroad, 1984.

Scott, Martin. *Sophia and the Johannine Jesus.* Journal for the Study of the Old Testament, Supplement Series 212. Sheffield: Sheffield Academic Press, 1992.

Segovia, Fernando F. "The Journey(s) of the Word: A Reading of the Plot of the Fourth Gospel." *Semeia* 53 (1991): 23–54.

Segovia, Fernando F. (ed.). *"What Is John?" Readers and Readings of the Fourth Gospel.* Symposium Series 3. Atlanta: Scholars Press, 1996.

Segovia, Fernando F. (ed.). *"What Is John?" Volume II, Literary and Social Readings of the Fourth Gospel.* Atlanta: Society of Biblical Literature, 1998.

Segovia, Fernando F. "Inclusion and Exclusion in John 17: An Intercultural Reading." In *"What Is John?" Vol. II, Literary and Social Readings of the Fourth Gospel*, edited by Fernando F. Segovia, Symposium Series, 281–322. Atlanta: Society of Biblical Literature, 1998.

Segovia, Fernando F. *Decolonizing Biblical Studies.* Maryknoll, NY: Orbis Books, 2000.

Segovia, Fernando F. "The Gospel of John." In *A Postcolonial Commentary on the New Testament Writings*, edited by Fernando F. Segovia and R. S. Sugirtharajah, 156–93. New York: T&T Clark, 2007.

Segovia, Fernando F. "Criticism in Critical Times: Reflections on Vision and Task." *Journal of Biblical Literature* 134, no. 1 (2015): 671–95.

Seim, Turid Karlsen. "Roles of Women in the Gospel of John." In *John and the Synoptics*, edited by Lars Hartman and Birger Olsson, 56–73. Uppsala: Almqvist & Wiksell, 1987.

Sheridan, Ruth. "Issues in the Translations of οἱ Ἰουδαῖοι in the Fourth Gospel." *Journal of Biblical Literature* 132, no. 3 (2013): 671–95.

Skinner, Christopher W. (ed.). *Characters and Characterization in the Gospel of John.* Library of New Testament Studies 416. London: Bloomsbury T&T Clark, 2014.

Smith, D. Moody. *John.* Abingdon New Testament Commentaries. Nashville, TN: Abingdon Press, 1999.

Stibbe, Mark W. G. *John as Storyteller.* Society for New Testament Monographs Series 73. Cambridge: Cambridge University Press, 1992.

Swanson, Tod D. "To Prepare a Place: Johannine Christianity and the Collapse of Ethnic Territory." In *John and Postcolonialism: Travel, Space and Power.*

The Bible and Postcolonialism, 7, edited by Musa W. Dube and Jeffrey Staley, 11–50. Sheffield: Sheffield Academic Press, 2002.

Talbert, Charles. *Reading John: A Literary and Theological Commentary on the Fourth Gospel and the Johannine Epistles*. Reading the New Testament Series. New York: Crossroad, 1992.

Tan, Yak-hwee. "The Johannine Community: Caught in 'Two Worlds.'" In *New Currents through John: A Global Perspective*, edited by Francisco Lozada Jr. and Tom Thatcher, 167–79. Atlanta: Society of Biblical Literature, 2006.

Taylor, Charles. *Multiculturalism: Examining the Politics of Recognition*. Princeton: Princeton University Press, 1994.

Thatcher, Tom. *Why John Wrote a Gospel: Jesus–Memory–History*. Louisville, KY: Westminster John Knox Press, 2006.

Thiselton, Anthony C. *Hermeneutics: An Introduction*. Grand Rapids, MI: Eerdmans, 2009.

Thompson, John B. T. *Studies in the Theory of Ideology*. Cambridge: Polity Press, 1984.

Tolbert, Mary Ann. "Writing History, Writing Culture, Writing Ourselves." In *Soundings in Cultural Criticism: Perspectives and Methods in Culture, Power, and Identity in the New Testament*, edited by Francisco Lozada Jr. and Greg Carey, 17–30. Minneapolis, MN: Fortress Press, 2013.

Trouillot, Michel-Rolph. *Silencing the Past: Power and the Production of History*. Boston: Beacon Press, 1995.

Author Index

Appleby, Joyce 9, 13, 24, 26, 101
Ashton, John 27, 101

Bauman, Zygmunt 9, 101
Benko, Andrew D. 9, 101
Bennema, Cornelis 56, 70, 72, 101
Brown, Raymond E. 4, 24–7, 57, 59, 67, 72–3, 84, 96, 101
Brown, Sherri 27, 71, 101
Bryant, Jo-Ann A. 26, 30, 53, 101
Bultmann, Rudolf 27, 101

Callahan, Allen Dwight 27, 101
Carter, Warren 16–17, 26, 30, 35, 39, 53, 101
Castles Stephen 101
Cohen, Shaye J. D. 58–9, 71, 101
Conway, Colleen M. 56, 61, 63, 71, 102
Culpepper, R. Alan 14–16, 26, 30–2, 53–4, 73, 84, 96, 102

de Boer, Martinus C. 84, 102
Dube, Musa W. 8, 25–7, 64, 71, 84, 102–3, 105

Estes, Douglas 54, 84, 102

Fehribach, Adeline 61, 66, 68, 71, 102
Fraser, Nancy 32, 53, 102

Gadamer, Hans-Georg 9, 102
Goss, Robert E. 72, 102
Guardiola-Sáenz, Letica A. 65, 71, 102
Gundry, Robert. H. 15, 26, 102

Hengel, Martin 27, 102
Honneth, Axel 32, 53, 102
Hunt, Lynn 9, 13, 24, 26, 101
Hylen, Susan E. 31, 38, 53, 56, 61, 66–7, 71, 102

Jacob, Margaret 9, 13, 24, 26, 101
Jeanrond, Werner 9, 103

Keener, Craig S. 27, 103
Kim, Jean Kim 64, 71, 103
Köstenberger, Andreas J. 27, 103
Kysar, Robert 27, 30, 53, 61, 68, 70–1, 97, 103
Kwok, Pui-lan 25, 103

Liew, Tat-Siong Benny 27, 103
Lozada Jr., Francisco 2, 4, 8, 22, 26–7, 31, 47, 53–4, 103, 106

Martínez, Oscar J. 9, 103
Martyn, J. Louis 4, 21–3, 26–7, 103
Miller, J. Maxwell 6, 8, 104
Miller, Mark J. 101
Moloney, Francis J. 30, 53, 73, 84, 96, 104
Myers, Alicia D. 56–7, 71, 104

O'Day, Gail 27, 104
Okure, Teresa 72, 104

Painter, John, R. 54, 84
Palmer, Richard E. 13, 26, 104
Powell, Mark Allan 17, 26, 104

Reinhartz, Adele 21–3, 26–7, 30, 53, 60, 71, 104
Resseguie, James L. 30, 53, 104

Schnackenburg , Rudolf 27, 104
Schneiders, Sandra M. 61, 69, 71, 105
Schüssler-Fiorenza, Elisabeth 71, 105
Scott, Martin 61, 71, 105
Segovia, Fernando F. 6, 8–9, 27–8, 30–1, 35, 53–4, 73–4, 84, 96, 104–5
Seim, Turid Karlsen 72, 105
Sheridan, Ruth. 59, 71, 105
Skinner, Christopher W. 27, 70–2, 101, 104–5

Smith, D. Moody 28, 105
Staley, Jeffrey L. 8, 27, 71, 84, 102–3, 105
Stibbe, Mark W. G. 30, 53, 105
Swanson, Tod D. 84, 105

Talbert, Charles 30, 54, 106
Tan, Yak-hwee 32, 54, 106
Taylor, Charles 9, 106
Thatcher, Tom 28, 103, 106
Thiselton, Anthony C. 27, 106
Thompson, John B. T. 8, 106
Tolbert, Mary Ann 6, 8, 106
Trouillot, Michel-Rolph 2, 4–5, 8, 106

Biblical Index

HEBREW BIBLE

Genesis
1   76, 77
1:1   75
24:11   63
29:2   63

Exodus
2:16   63
3:14   43
12:46   50

Leviticus
19:18   47

Numbers
9:12

Psalms
41:9   90

Zechariah
12:10   50
13:1   50

NEW TESTAMENT

Matthew
2:10   14
4:10   62
10:1-4   14
26:12   67

Mark
1:24   62
3:14-19   14
3:17   14
14:8   67

Luke
4:34   62
6:13-16   14
6:14   14

John
1-4   30
1:1   32, 74,
                     75, 83, 88
1:2   33, 75
1:1-2   32, 74
1:1-18   17, 25, 31,
                     32, 37, 73,
                     74, 83, 85
1:3   37, 76, 79
1:3-5   33
1:3-17   32, 33, 74, 76
1:4   78
1:4-5   37
1:5   77
1:6   35, 77
1:6-8   81
1:6-9   33
1:7   33, 77
1:8   33, 78
1:9   69, 78, 79
1:9-10   69
1:10   69, 70, 79

1:10-13	33	2:1-11	61
1:11	37, 79	2:1-12	24, 37, 62
1:12	79	2:4	42, 62
1:13	80, 81	2:5	62
1:14	14, 37, 80, 81	2:6	58
1:14-17	34	2:7	62
1:15	81	2:9	62
1:16	81	2:11	62
1:17	34, 82	2:12	31, 37, 61
1:18	32, 34, 74, 82	2:13	38
1:19	35, 57	2:13-31	35
1:19-28	78	2:13–3:21	38
1:19-51	61	2:15	38
1:19-34	35	2:16	38
1:19–3:36	31, 35, 39, 61	2:18	38
1:19–17:26	31, 35, 74	2:19	38
1:20	36	2:20	58
1:23	38	3	63
1:24	35, 36	3:1	63
1:28	31	3:1-21	25, 38
1:29	36, 50	3:2	63
1:30	36	3:3	39
1:29-34	20	3:8	39
1:32-34	36	3:8-9	38
1:34	36	3:10-15	39
1:35-41	24	3:16	39, 70, 89
1:35-51	37	3:17	39, 70
1:35–2:12	35	3:22	31, 35
1:36	31, 36	3:22-26	25, 35, 55
1:40	15	3:30	20
1:41	36, 42, 66	3:32-36	39
1:43	36	4	63
1:43-51	36	4:1–5:47	31
1:45	36	4:1-42	20, 63
1:47-48	40	4:1-54	39
1:48-49	37, 64	4:3-4	31
1:49	66	4:4-44	24
1:50-51	37	4:6	63
2	63	4:7	63
2:1	36, 61	4:9	40, 64
2:3	62	4:10	40
2:4	62, 87	4:11	64

4:12	64	6:48	43
4:15	40	6:51	43
4:16-18	40, 63	6:53-59	43
4:16-19	63	6:60-61	43
4:19-26	64	6:60-69	25
4:19-42	64	6:66	43
4:20	64	6:66-71	43
4:28	64	6:69	66
4:29	66	7	43
4:39-42	40, 64	7:1	57
4:42	24	7:1-9	43
4:43-54	40	7:3-5	25
4:46-54	24	7:4	70
5	42	7:6	87
5-19	30	7:7	70
5:1	57	7:8	87
5:1-9	24, 41	7:10	43
5:1-47	40	7:10–8:59	45
5:9	41, 44	7:10–10:42	43
5:10	57, 59	7:13	59
5:14	18	7:20	43
5:15	59	7:32	44
5:18	21, 24, 41, 42, 57, 59	7:35	24
		7:43	44
5:19-47	41	7:44	44
5:37	57, 59	7:50	63
5:45	57	7:51	44
6:1-2	42	7:53–8:11	25, 44, 65
6:1–10:42	31, 42	8:7-9	65
6:1-13	24	8:11	66
6:6-66	25	8:12	43, 44, 70
6:10	42	8:12-59	44
6:14-15	42	8:20	87
6:15	42	8:23	44
6:15-25	24	8:31	25
6:16-21	43	8:44	2, 44, 57
6:20	42	8:58-59	21
6:22-65	43	8:59	44
6:33-35	43	9:1-7	24
6:35	43	9:1-41	44
6:41	43	9:1–10:42	45
6:41-52	43	9:5	43, 44

9:7	44	12:1-11	22
9:13	44	12:6	67
9:18	44	12:7	46
9:22	18, 21, 57, 59	12:9	57
9:24-34	44	12:9-11	46
9:34	21	12:11	22
9:39	25	12:12-19	46
10:1-21	45	12:12-50	46
10:7	43	12:12–17:26	46
10:9	43	12:20-22	20
10:11	43	12:20-23	24
10:12	25	12:20-26	46
10:14	43	12:23	87
10:16	18	12:27	87
10:33	21	12:27-36	46
10:36	92	12:31	25, 70, 87
10:42	45	12:35-36	25
11-12	58	12:36	46
11:1	31	12:37-42	24, 47
11:1-44	22, 24, 45	12:42	18, 21
11:1-46	66	12:44-50	47
11:1–12:10	45	13:1	87, 90
11:1–17:26	31, 45	13:1-17	47
11:16	51	13:1-30	47
11:19	22	13:1–16:33	87
11:20	66	13:1–17:26	47, 86
11:21	66	13:4	67
11:21-22	45	13:8-30	47
11:25	43, 46	13:23-24	14
11:26	46	13:31	87
11:27	46, 66	13:31-32	47
11:28	46	13:31–16:33	87
11:31	67	13:33	47
11:32	46, 66	13:36-38	47
11:33	67	14:1-14	47
11:35	67	14:3	47
11:39	46	14:5	51
11:45	57	14:6	43, 48
11:51-52	46	14:12	48
11:53	46	14:14	91
11:55–12:11	46	14:15-31	48
12:1-8	66, 67	14:22	48

15:1	43	17:17	92
15:1-17	48	17:18	92
15:5	43	17:19	89, 92
15:11	91	17:20	92, 93
15:12	47	17:20-21	93
15:17	47	17:20-26	49, 86,
15:18–16:4	48		87, 92, 93
16:1-4	21	17:21	87, 93
16:2	18	17:22	93
16:4-15	48	17:23	93
16:16-24	48	17:24	69, 87, 93, 94
16:20	70	17:25	87, 94
16:22	91	17:26	94
16:24	91	18:1-3	49
16:25-33	48	18:1-12	49
16:32	48	18:1–19:16	49
16:33	70	18:1–20:25	87
17:1	87	18:1–21:25	31, 49,
17:1-3	88		52, 61, 74
17:1-5	49, 86,	18:4	49
	87, 87, 93	18:10-12	49
17:1-26	85	18:13-27	49
17:2	87, 88, 89	18:28–19:16	50
17:2-3	88	19:4	68
17:3	92	19:7	57, 59
17:4	88	19:15	57
17:4-5	88, 93	19:17	50
17:5	69, 87, 88	19:19	50
17:6	89	19:17-37	45, 50
17:6-9	86	19:17-42	50
17:6-19	49, 87, 92, 93	19:20	50
17:7	89	19:25-26	50
17:7-8	89	19:25-28	61
17:9	89	19:25-30	68
17:10	89	19:30	50
17:11	87, 90, 93	19:31	50
17:11-12	90	19:31-34	50
17:12	90	19:35	14, 50
17:13	90	19:36-37	50
17:14	91	19:38	63
17:15	91, 95	19:38-42	50
17:16	91, 94	20-21	30

20:1	51	21:1	31
20:1-10	50, 68	21:1-8	24
20:1-18	67	21:1-25	51, 52
20:1–21:25	50	21:2	14
20:2	67, 68	21:4	68
20:2-10	14	21:7	14, 52
20:3-5	51	21:12	52
20:9	68	2:13	52
20:10	51	21:15-17	52
20:11	51	21:15-19	52
20:11-18	68	21:20-23	25
20:11-31	50	21:20-24	14
20:14	51	21:24	14, 52
20:15	68	21:25	52, 69
20:16	51	21:24-25	14
20:17	68		
20:18	51, 68	*Acts of Apostles*	
20:19	51	18-19	17
20:19-23	51	18:24-26	17
20:19-23	51	19:1-7	17
20:21	51	19:11-16	17
20:22-23	51		
20:24-29	51, 68	*1 John*	15
20:25	62		
20:27	51	*2 John*	15
20:28	51		
20:30	51	*3 John*	15
20:30-31	23, 52		
20:31	19, 52	*Revelation*	
21	25	1:9	14, 15

Subject Index

adulterous woman 65–6
Andrew 36, 42, 66
authorship 2, 11–17, 19, 20, 25, 29, 56, 58, 69

Beloved Disciple 14, 15, 20, 24–5, 50–2, 62, 67–9
blind man 21, 44–5, 55
border 7, 31, 24, 41, 74, 97
borderlands 97–9

community 1, 4, 8, 12, 16, 18, 20–4, 26, 32, 36–7, 39–41, 44–5, 48–9, 56–7, 63–4, 66–8, 72, 74, 79–82, 86–95
cosmos 1, 32, 34, 58, 69
crowd 42–3, 46, 57

dating 13, 17–9, 25, 29
disciples 16–17, 21, 36–8, 42–3, 47–52, 55, 58, 61–2, 66, 68, 86–7, 89–94
dualism 7, 12, 24, 30–1, 33–5, 52, 59–60, 78–9, 82–3, 85, 90–1, 94

hermeneutics 1, 3–4, 6, 11, 13, 17, 98
historical 1–3, 5–7, 11–17, 19, 21–5, 27, 29–30, 56, 59, 62, 86, 97–8
history 1–6, 13, 15–17, 19–21, 23–6, 29, 56, 59–60, 63, 65, 83, 85, 97–9

identity 12–16, 18, 20–3, 26, 31–52, 55, 57, 60, 62–4, 66, 68, 70, 74–6, 79–81, 93–4, 97
ideological 1–2, 5–7, 12, 15, 23, 26, 31–2, 56, 60–1, 66, 73, 75, 86, 98

John the Baptist 20, 24–5, 33–5, 66, 77, 81
Jews, the 2, 18, 21–6, 35, 38, 40–6, 49–51, 53, 55–61, 63, 65, 67, 69–70
Judas 67, 90

lame man 40–1, 44
Lazarus 22, 45–6, 66–7
literary 1, 3–7, 12, 23, 29–31, 33, 35, 37, 39, 41, 43, 45, 47, 49, 51, 55–6, 59–62, 66, 69, 73, 86, 97–8
literary criticism 5, 29
Logos 17, 33, 69, 70, 74–5

Martha 22, 45–6, 66–7, 83
Mary (of Bethany) 22, 45–6, 66–7, 83
Mary Magdalene 50–1, 67–9
Mary (wife of Clopas) 50
mother (of Jesus) 37, 43, 48, 50, 61–3, 67–8, 83

narrative 1–8, 14, 17, 19, 20, 22–3, 25, 29, 30–5, 37, 39, 43–6, 49, 50–2, 59, 60–3, 65, 67–9, 73–4, 83, 85–6, 98
narrativization 1, 4–5, 30, 98
Nathanael 36–7, 64, 66
Nicodemus 25, 38–40, 44, 50, 63

other (the) 12, 32, 53, 59, 66, 89, 90–2, 94, 99

Peter 20, 25, 36, 42–3, 47, 49–52, 66–8
Pharisees 21, 25, 35, 44, 46–7, 59
Pilate 50

plot 1, 5, 30–2, 35–6, 39, 49, 52, 57–8, 61,
  73–4, 77–8, 87, 89
prayer 21, 49, 69, 85–7, 89, 90–5
provenance 13, 16–17, 19, 25, 29
purpose (of gospel) 13, 19–20, 25, 29,
  77–8, 90, 93–4

recognition (motif) 30–53, 55, 62, 64–5,
  67–8, 74, 77–9, 95

representation 1–3, 7–8, 22, 32, 56, 59,
  60–4, 66, 70, 76, 83, 87

Samaritan woman 24, 39–41, 43, 63–4,
  66, 69, 83

theological 11, 12, 15, 18, 23, 33, 60, 64,
  70, 74–5, 86, 97